# CAZÚ ZEGERS

## Architecture in Poetic Territories

To Clara & Godo

# CAZÚ ZEGERS

## Architecture in Poetic Territories

Philip Jodidio

Ces poètes seront ! Quand sera brisé l'infini servage de la femme, quand elle vivra pour elle et par elle, l'homme, jusqu'ici abominable, — lui ayant donné son renvoi, elle sera poète, elle aussi ! La femme trouvera de l'inconnu ! Ses mondes d'idées différeront-ils des nôtres ? — Elle trouvera des choses étranges, insondables, repoussantes, délicieuses ; nous les prendrons, nous les comprendrons.

Arthur Rimbaud, *Lettre du Voyant*, à Paul Demeny, 15 mai 1871

These poets will exist! When at last the infinite servitude of women is broken, when women will live for and of themselves, and when man who has been abominable until now – has given her his dismissal, she too will be a poet! Woman will find the unknown! Will her worlds of ideas be different from ours? She will find strange, unfathomable, repulsive, and delicious things – we will accept them, we will understand.

Arthur Rimbaud, *Second Letter of the Seer*, to Paul Demeny, May 15, 1871

# Table of Contents

08 From the Word
to the Territory
The Work of Cazú Zegers
Philip Jodidio

18 Thesis
on Territory
Cazú Zegers

20 I.
Concrete
Capilla Espíritu Santo
Casa Do
Casa Soplo

72 II.
Timber
Casa Esmeralda
Casa Ye
Casa Lum

120 III.
Hospitality
Hotel Tierra Patagonia
Hotel Magnolia
Family Lodge Casa Llu
Family Lodge Casa del Fuego
Family Lodge Casa Pyr

206 IV.
Tiny Projects
Pueblo

216 V.
Geopoetics
The territory is to America what
monuments are to Europe
Cazú Zegers

225 VI.
Projects Technical Details

251 VII.
Acknowledgments

# From the Word to the Territory

The Work of Cazú Zegers

▲ **Casa Granero (2004)**
Kawelluco, Araucanía Region, Chile.
Photos ©Guy Wenborne

The Chilean architect Cazú Zegers calls her projects "Prototypes in Territories," referring to her search for a language of Latin American forms. What characterizes her projects is the "conceptual movement generated by crossing from the *poetic word*, to the *inhabitant* and finally to the territory, which generates a *gesture* that unfolds in space." This method allows Zegers to move through different scales— from object (micro) to territory (macro) and back again. She has also called her work "geopoetry," where the close relationship among territory, community, and architecture is expressed. Early examples involving "a syncretism between ancestral techniques and contemporary architecture in wood" include her design for six houses in Kawelluco, Chile (1995–2004). These were the Fogón House (1997), Santa María House (1998), Silencio House (1999), Casa Taller Cubo (1999), Cáscara House (2002), Té 1A House (2002), and the more widely published Granero House (2004). Kawelluco, a former logging area, is now a 2,470-acre (1,000-hectare) nature park. The park and the small nearby city of Pucón in the central lake area of Chile fall under the shadow of the active Villarrica volcano. Zegers imagines her houses as part of a ruralization as opposed to an urbanization—each residence has at least two and a half acres (a hectare) of land, and the plans conceptualize the idea that "Villarrica could destroy the area again and again." In collaboration with residents, the architect developed two types of low-budget house built by local carpenters. As it happens, the approach Zegers used twenty years ago has become very popular with today's young Chilean architects. Another early work is her Cala House (Ranco Lake, Región de Los Ríos, Chile, 1992), which was intended as an echo of local vernacular architecture and specifically the wooden sheds built by German settlers in the area. Her "deconstruction" of the design of these sheds allowed her to reassemble their constituent elements in a new form, thus inhabiting the regional landscape in a contemporary way.

Born in 1958, Cazú Zegers (given name María del Carmen Zegers) studied architecture at the Universidad Católica de Valparaíso (UCV), graduating in 1984. She traveled widely after graduating, then worked in the office of the architect Delgado Gilbride and at Juan Pablo Molyneux Studio in New York (1987–88) before founding her own practice in 1990 in Santiago. Her production has ranged from architecture to furniture and lamp design, but she has also ventured into urban and cultural planning, as well as territorial management. She considers her industrial design, interiors, larger buildings, and single-family homes to "highlight the search for new architectural forms generated through the relationship between poetry and architecture." She has concentrated on low technology or Low Tech. Her work is largely in wood but also includes some remarkable concrete structures such as the Holy Spirit Chapel (Puente Alto, Santiago, Chile, 2003) and the Breath House (Lo Barnechea, Santiago, 2011). Her Tierra Patagonia Hotel (Torres del Paine, Región de Magallanes y Antártica Chilena, Chile, 2011) received a 2013 Wallpaper Design Award for Best New Hotel, while her Magnolia Hotel (Santiago, Chile, 2016) took on the complex renovation and expansion of an existing building. As this book went to press, Zegers had completed twenty-four single-family houses and was starting work on four more. She has also realized twenty-six projects of other types.

## The Open City

Zegers's interest in territory and history directly relate to her experience as a student: "My primary influence in Chile and Latin America was my architecture school, with its poetic vision and the experimental Ciudad Abierta [Open City] of Amereida." The Open City is located north of Valparaíso on the Pacific coast in nearly 670 acres (a 270-hectare area) of dunes, wetlands, and pine forest. The site was purchased by the university in 1970, and it became the location for a heterogeneous group of more than forty structures—including open spaces (*agoras*), workshops, living spaces (*hospederías* and *cubículas*), places of worship, and sculptures.

The idea for the project took root in 1969 under the leadership of the architect Alberto Cruz Covarrubias (1917–2013) and the poet Godofredo Iommi Marini (1917–2001). A research group emerged around them, in which young professionals shared the belief that a different type of architecture could arise from a new way of life, which would stem naturally from a poetic conception of their homeland—America. In a 1984 text on the Open City, Cruz, inspired by Iommi, wrote, "We have decided to become naked in front of the poetic word. It warns us, with

▲ **Casa Cala (1992)**
Lago Ranco, Región de Los Ríos, Chile.
Photo ©Cristina Alemparte

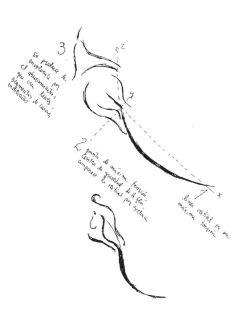

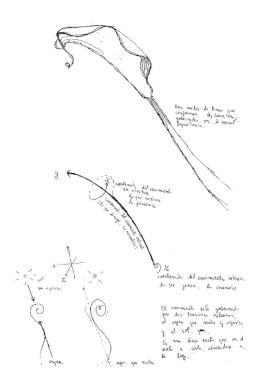

Rimbaud, that word and action no longer rhyme as in the time of the Greeks, that they will not rhyme anymore, words will precede action. This opens a gap under our feet. And at this moment, we seek to build a dialogue with the craftsmen of architecture through that gap."

It was no accident that the poet Iommi, an Argentine whose parents were of Italian origin, became the spiritual leader of the group. Cruz suggested that by citing Arthur Rimbaud and his *Second Letter of the Seer* (May 15, 1871) the new architecture he envisaged would be first and foremost poetic but would also be the fruit of a very practical type of interdisciplinary collaboration.

> Cet avenir sera matérialiste, vous le voyez ; — Toujours pleins du *Nombre* et de l'*Harmonie* ces poèmes seront faits pour rester. — Au fond, ce serait encore un peu la Poésie grecque.
>
> L'art éternel aurait ses fonctions ; comme les poètes sont citoyens. La Poésie ne rhythmera plus l'action, elle *sera en avant*.

> This future will be materialistic, as you see. — Always filled with Number and Harmony, these poems will be made to endure. — Fundamentally, it would be Greek poetry again in a new way.
>
> Eternal art would have its functions since poets are citizens. Poetry will not lend its rhythm to action; it will be in advance.

Other members of the Amereida group admired by Zegers include the Chilean architects Manuel Casanueva Carrasco (1943–2014) and Miguel Eyquem Astorga (1922–2021), who said that the spirit of the Open City was "a life experience . . ." and proclaimed: "Let us get rid of all the isms in the world and all the religions. We are discovering who we are." Zegers says that other Latin American influences marked her formative years—from the Incan and Mayan cultures to the architecture of Luis Barragán (1902–1988) and Eladio Dieste (1917–2000). Dieste was in fact a Uruguayan engineer who used what he called reinforced ceramics—employed in light vaulted structures made of brick, steel, and a minimal amount of concrete. The fact that she highlights Dieste emphasizes Zegers's deep interest in the materiality of her own architecture.

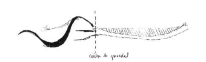

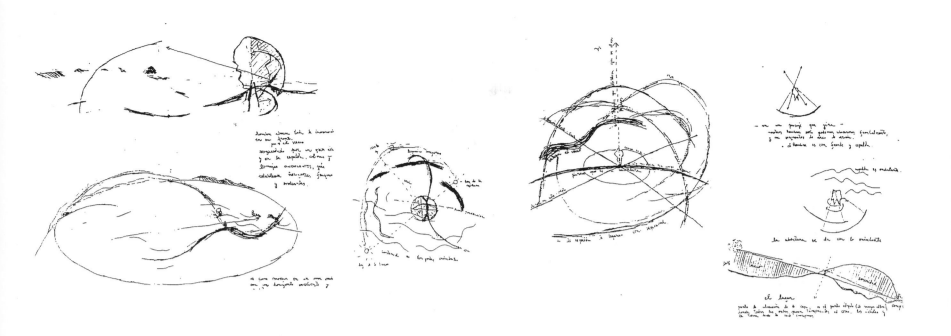

▲ **Original Sketches of Casa Cala (1991)**
Gesture-Figure-Form Methodology ©Cazú Zegers

## Compressed yet Endless

But Zegers was from a newer generation than the founders of the Open City—and she wanted to look even further afield for her inspiration. "At that time," she says, "they [the founders of the Open City] didn't have originals, and there were no imports, so they created everything!" Her path was not quite the same. She recalls visiting New York for the first time in 1984: "I will never forget the emotion I had when I reached Manhattan, directly through Penn Station. I was with my sister Marcela, and I spoke to her about the impressive, compressed yet endless space opening to the sky." This trip was when Zegers first saw paintings by Zaha Hadid and fashion designs by Rei Kawakubo (Comme des Garçons). From New York, she extended her first voyage out of Latin America with a trip to Europe accompanied by her sister. With Eurail passes, the pair spent six months seeing as much as they could—from the buildings of Antoni Gaudí to the Parthenon. By this time, Zegers had completed her studies, where she had been attracted to the work of no less than "Le Corbusier, Frank Lloyd Wright, Mies van der Rohe, Philip Johnson (Glass House), the Bauhaus, Frei Otto, and the Futurists." What's more, she says, "As a young architect I deeply admired Tadao Ando."

In fact, the breadth and depth of Zegers's artistic and architectural observations speak directly to her engagement and interest as an architect. She is an admirer of the American artist Richard Serra, but also of the Chilean sculptor Marta Colvin Andrade (1907–1995), the daughter of Irish and Portuguese immigrants. "Trips have strongly influenced me, as you can see, I am an adventurous spirit," says Zegers. But this broader reflection on her sources of inspiration brings Zegers back to what she considers essential: "It is an endless list," she says, "but what still marks me the most is the Latin American territory and vernacular cultures. As an architecture student, I did three off-road motorcycle trips covering all of Chile, from the north to the south. It was what I would call a pre-developed country, so there was little more than local culture. Traveling on a small motorcycle, you can't carry much, only a tent, and some gear for the rain and the cold. My boyfriend's motorcycle carried the gas. There weren't even gas stations or hotels to pass the night. So, I always say that in these trips, that is when the territory entered my soul, and that's what my architecture is about."

In her lengthy list of cultural references, books like Ayn Rand's *The Fountainhead* (1943) and György Dóczi's *The Power of Limits: Proportional Harmonies in Nature, Art, and Architecture* (1981) stand out, but there are also influences that emerge more strongly in her built work. One of these is Japan. If she thinks of Tadao Ando's powerful geometry or the flowing garments of Issey Miyake, Zegers also cites Jun'ichirō Tanizaki's book *In Praise of Shadows* (1933), which traces the subtle, deep links between the culture of the past and the present in Japan. "I feel that my work has always resonated with Japanese aesthetics, to the point that I believe in another incarnation I must have been Japanese."

## In the Beginning was the Word

Always and again the thoughts of Zegers return to her native Chile, to its landscape and from there to its vernacular architecture, but also to its literature and poetry, in particular *Altazor o el viaje en paracaídas* (1919–31), a poem in seven cantos written by Vicente Huidobro (1893–1948). *Altazor* is a combination of the words *altura* (altitude) and *azorado* (astonishment or bewilderment), corresponding to the subtleties and expressive possibilities of the Spanish language, which play a clear part not only in the names of the architect's projects but also in their form and substance. Huidobro's *creacionismo* (creationism) sought the development of a new form of poetic expression, focusing on the word as the building block of creation, and from there to imagining worlds that may not be a pure reflection of nature. And so, the references of Zegers return to Rimbaud and the Amereida, but also perhaps to one book that she does not specifically cite—the Bible: "In the beginning was the Word, and the Word was with God, and the Word was God" (John 1:1).

## Paradigm Shift

The wide-ranging curiosity of Zegers has led her to focus on such unexpected subjects as the work of Godfrey Reggio, an American director of experimental documentary films. In 2020 when she was the Saarinen Visiting Professor at the Advanced Design Studio of the Yale School of Architecture, she used Reggio's film *Koyaanisqatsi: Life Out of Balance* (1982) to posit the emergence of a new cultural paradigm in which she opposes the Americanized and "the Pacifiers." The 1982 film is a "visual tone-poem" with music by Philip Glass that explores the relationship between cities and the natural environment in the United States. Zegers includes the Americas, and her native Chile, in her definition, when she states, "We Americans need to reconnect with our origin, return to the land and understand it as sacred, to learn from its Indigenous communities that it is sustainable in and of itself. The human species belongs to the land; we cannot develop life separated from it."

It may be useful to recall that ideas about the relation between territory and architecture in the 1980s were not uniquely Chilean. In his 1982 book, *The Architecture of the City*, the Italian architect Aldo Rossi wrote, "The history of the city is always inseparable from its geography." But it is clear that Zegers is referring to concepts that go beyond her personal experience, striving for an approach that can be considered universal. "This means that the territory where we are born shapes our being. We face the urgency of reconnecting, to open new narratives about the territory that will allow us, in time, to build healthy cities, rebalancing life in a post-technological world.

◄ **Andes Workshop (2017)**
First version of the workshop in Mirador Patachoique, Araucanía Region, Chile. Photos by student Lore Mellado

This paradigm shift is necessarily accompanied by incorporating the attributes of the feminine and Indigenous communities into the cultural process."

She has taken these ideas into the real world not only with her architectural practice but also with such initiatives as the Andes Workshop, which she founded in 2016 with Grupo Talca. Martín del Solar and Rodrigo Sheward created the experimental team Grupo Talca in 2003, which believes "in the importance of architecture transcending the intellectual dimension and reconnecting with the body." The workshop offers attendees a two-month opportunity to develop and build a project where "territorial, landscape and environmental themes are the basis to integrate communities and their trades."

### Aspects of the Being

Zegers has for a number of years given what she calls poetic names or words as clues to her projects. Her own house, called Soplo (Lo Barnechea, Metropolitan Region, Santiago de Chile, 2011), is indeed like a breath of fresh air. The word *soplo* means "to blow," or "to murmur." As she says, "It is the wind that gently passes and leaves its trace on sand or snow." It was created to liberate the "feminine aspects of the being." Zegers does not suggest an active opposition between men and women in the field of architecture. And yet in a conversation with the architect, she unexpectedly said, "I have a lot of water in me." Asked to define this idea, she says:

> Water has to do with emotions. There are men who have a strong sensitivity—but it has to do with how one approaches a project. I like to speak about the aspects of a being, and I do not like to specifically oppose men and women. Men occupy space and sometimes do not recognize that the ideas come from women. I have been speaking to the Mexican architects Frida Escobedo and Tatiana Bilbao. Their education is more Anglo-Saxon than mine. Here, when you are born, they teach you that you need a man to take care of you—we are all looking for the charming prince; but this has to do with culture and not with the aspects of the being. I believe that women are becoming more secure and comfortable in what they can do. Architecture is difficult—it requires a very strong will to get projects done. When I went to school, our teachers thought that women could not be architects because we did not have the mental structure required. My approach was to say, yes, this is true, but we have other ways to design. This reference may indeed come back to Rimbaud's *Second Letter of the Seer*. I would say that architecture is a mixture of culture, sensibility, and where you place your goals. Perhaps men are more focused on recognition. Women want mainly to do good projects—to make a space for people. I was often the only woman in my class. My teacher, Godofredo Iommi, though, created a distinction and created a group called Poetic Acts—he said that Latino men did not have the voice to read it. In a symbolic sense my teacher gave me a voice. Our voice is of course different from that of men. Women look in a different way and we are open in other ways—I would say that that is very important in my work. I am and have been for a very long time, perhaps since my childhood, extremely concerned about the climate and the need to be sustainable. I believe that poetry can open us to the unknown and I am trying to bring forward that which is unknown.[1]

> *Ces poètes seront ! Quand sera brisé l'infini servage de la femme, quand elle vivra pour elle et par elle, l'homme, jusqu'ici abominable, — lui ayant donné son renvoi, elle sera poète, elle aussi ! La femme trouvera de l'inconnu ! Ses mondes d'idées différeront-ils des nôtres ? — Elle trouvera des choses étranges, insondables, repoussantes, délicieuses ; nous les prendrons, nous les comprendrons.*

> These poets will exist! When at last the infinite servitude of women is broken, when women will live for and of themselves, and when man who has been abominable until now—has given her his dismissal, she too will be a poet! Woman will find the unknown! Will her worlds of

▲ **Cazú Zegers in Casa Soplo (2023)**
Photo ©Cristóbal Palma

[1] This quote and others from the text: Cazú Zegers in conversation with the author, August 8, 2023.

ideas be different from ours? She will find strange, unfathomable, repulsive, and delicious things—we will accept them, we will understand.

Arthur Rimbaud, *Second Letter of the Seer*, May 15, 1871

## Energy and Transformation of the Word

As in the Gospel according to John, Zegers says, "The poetic word is what comes at the beginning of the artistic process. It's what makes the project what it is. I like to have some mystery, but the poetic word is a clue to a project." When she names her project, it has not yet materialized, but the poetic word exists—*fuego* (fire), for example. Zegers explains:

> The architecture is of course made of space, light, and materials, but the poetry involves adding the territory and the presence of the clients. I have also added energy in the sense of Einstein's celebrated formula to the list of what makes up a house, or architecture in general. When I created the Casa Fuego [House of Fire], I was thinking of a spiral galaxy. This brought attributes to the project, which evolves from its center—I want architecture that is dynamic and not static. What I bring to the project is a play on limits—what is within and what is out. There are continual relations created between the inside and the exterior, but it is not as though there are very formal limits.

The play on interior and exterior is of course an essential element of Japanese architecture where the *engawa*, or covered passage, is by definition neither inside nor outside. The climate of much of Chile facilitates a free communication between what is enclosed and what is open, but Zegers insists:

> The blurring of the distinctions between inside and out may sometimes be easier in the climate of Chile, but if you think of Patagonia, it is very cold there. The Tierra Patagonia Hotel [Sarmiento Lake, Torres del Paine, Magallanes Region, 2011] is an enclosed building, but it also has a strong relation with the landscape. It is very much a question of the relation between the building and its territory—of the dialogue between architecture and territory. The Magnolia Hotel [Santiago, 2016] has to do with the restoration or reuse of architectural patrimony. It is a matter of working with tradition more than it is about reanimating an old building. There is a resonance between the old and the new that has to do with materials. The new material is glass, which allows light through its transparency to penetrate the exterior from within. We brought more light into the space than the original building had in this way as well. The poetry has to do with adding contemporary elements to tradition. But it is clear that tradition is the starting point. I took a photo of light reflecting on a lake that symbolizes my action here—we brought light to patios or courtyards that existed but which had little light. You feel that you are in an atmosphere.

Zegers points out that her thinking about transparency, and one might also say her attachment to the power of poetry, comes in part from the Italian writer Italo Calvino (1923–1985), who affirmed a "list of values to be saved" in his *Six Memos for the Next Millennium*. This book, cut short by the death of the author, was written for the 1985–86 Charles Eliot Norton Lectures at Harvard University but first published in 1988. Calvino wrote, "If I have included *visibility* in my list of values to be saved, it is to give a warning of the danger we run in losing a basic human faculty, the power to bring visions into focus with our eyes, of bringing forth forms and colors from the lines of black letters on a white page, and in fact *thinking* in terms of images." The connection that Zegers makes between the poetic word and architecture is precisely about the act of "bringing forth forms and colors from the lines of black letters on a white page . . ."

Though it is situated in central Santiago, the Magnolia Hotel is connected to a broader territory, which goes beyond the city streets and urban development. Zegers continues:

I made a terrace on the top of the hotel that gives views of all the main mountains of Santiago. Here, you experience space as a metaphysical territory. I think that everyone can feel this in some way—but it does depend on how sensitive you are. As the Chilean philosopher and biologist Ricardo Rozzi says, we grow with the landscape into which we are born, and the territory is a bridge between nature and society that implies a reference to Indigenous heritage. Each place has its own relation to the land—it has to do with culture. The place you will go and the people who will speak about their land allow you to understand the territory even if it is not your native country. It is about a sense of the place. Architects are like interpreters.

From the terrace of the Magnolia Hotel, the Cerro El Plomo—the highest mountain visible from Santiago and a sacred place for the Incas—comes into view. The nearby Plaza de Armas was built in line with the summer solstice over an Incan square that was also aligned on the Apu Plomo, which the Inca considered to be a living god. Zegers says, "You can see these mountains from the roof terrace. I hope that one day we will fully understand their importance." Although naming and understanding the historic significance of these mountains is not obvious for some, the facts underlying these territorial presences give substance and weight to Zegers's reasoning. As much as contemporary society may cast aside knowledge of the past, or rather leave it to sources on the Internet, the underlying presence of Incan culture, or the alignment of the summer solstice are incontrovertible.

## Spiritual and Material

While Zegers underlines her own connection to the land and culture of Chile, she insists that the comprehension of territory she espouses allows not only for many interpretations but also for multiple locations. "I feel that architecture is universal—my interpretation or that of another person adds another layer to the project, but it is not the essential element," she says. In fact, it may be the idea of territory that is universal as much as any architectural form. Zegers fully accepts that territory can imply a mental space, or indeed a metaphysical space. She says, "The most metaphysical space in Chile is Patagonia—it is both spiritual and material."

Asked if her concept of territory can readily be transposed to other places that she does not know in such an instinctive and deep way, she says, "I was asked to create a geopoetic house for the Scottish poet Kenneth White in the Ardèche region of France, but he died this year." White invented the concept of geopoetics, whose basis was to "reestablish and enrich the long-severed man-earth relationship," and he owned a farm in a place called Gourgounel in the Beaume valley of Ardèche. For Zegers, who was about to visit Ardèche as this text was being prepared, it was clear that she would be able to understand those elements of territory that make this southern French region so particular, all the more that she was going on a search for the very origins of geopoetics.

## A Liberated Spirit

Though her work seems spacious, bright, and connected to the earth, Zegers's practice has not always been free of controversy: "My architecture has long been considered avant-garde in Chile, and for a long time, most of my projects were rejected." Queried about the more precise reasons for this rejection, which surely goes beyond a perception of excessive modernity, she explains, "I start with the word and create spaces that confront people in their spirit, in their being. Sometimes that makes people uncomfortable. When my mother decided to build the Emerald House [Casa Esmeralda, Lo Barnechea, Santiago, 2014], she was seventy-six years old, and she wanted to have a different life. I designed a house that had completely open space, which is entirely related to the territory. When my mother first encountered the house, she entered it as a very formal person, and now she is wild. She is still very elegant, but she is wild. The space allowed her to fundamentally be what she is; it liberated her. If others live in the house later, it will be because the space speaks to them."

Though she does not declare that architecture can change the world, Zegers is nonetheless convinced that some of her works have had an impact on the world of real users. She states, "The church that I did [Holy Spirit Chapel, Puente Alto, Santiago, 2003] at first met with opposition—church officials asked why they should build a church like this in a poor community—they thought it better to build in harmony with the poverty of the place. I responded that on the contrary, poverty implied that the church should be remarkable, a place where people could go to feel better, to feel that they are important. When the church was finished, young people kissed the walls because they said it gave them confidence that they could change their lives."

## I've Seen Fire and I've Seen Rain

Zegers's sketches and plans demonstrate the extent to which she is capable of adapting her creativity to location, function, and the specific poetic word she employs at the outset of each project. She explains in the case of the Llu House Family Lodge [Casa Llu Family Lodge, Maihue Lake, Los Ríos Region, Chile, 2018] that the house is in a very rainy area, "a condition that evokes a poetic word for architectural design as *a cloak of protection from the rain*. This is a reference to precarious tents that lumberjacks make in the forest with nylon stretched by wires, sometimes with a central pillar to let the water run down." She goes on to affirm that "*water* is the second poetic word that guides the design. This leads to the study of the geometric composition of water molecules; thus, the idea of three bodies ($H_2O$) connected to each other guides the floor plan made up of one level of connected space under a great blanket of protection against the rain, a cover made in handcrafted Corten steel." Climate, local tradition, and even the molecular composition of water enter her thought process—as well as the final forms of the house.

## The Language of Sensitivity

Zegers says that the poet Godofredo Iommi gave her *her* voice when he told a class composed mostly of men that only a woman could read poetry like that of Rimbaud aloud. And this is surely why the architect centers the poetic word at the beginning of each project—it is the hidden clue, as she says, something that is profound and linked not only to the precise circumstances of a house, but also to its territory in the metaphysical sense. After so many years of allowing finance and the reputation of the architect to guide and form buildings, Zegers instead begins with the poetic word *water*, which also connects, as she explains, to emotions—her emotions and those of others as well. She makes no claim to be better than her male counterparts, but she does affirm her own voice. "She will find strange, unfathomable, repulsive, and delicious things—we will accept them, we will understand," wrote Rimbaud.

Beginning with the experiment of the Open City and its affirmation that new architecture could arise from the poetic expression of the land, the earth, the territory, and deeply connected to her own homeland—and to its vast, metaphysical spaces like Patagonia—Zegers did not hesitate to look further: north, west, and east. What do Rei Kawakubo, Issey Miyake, and *In Praise of Shadows* have to do with an architect born in Chile? Perhaps everything, but especially a shared and common sensitivity to the way things are, to the value of what seems ephemeral and for some, meaningless. To deconstruct vernacular architecture (originated by German settlers in Chile) and to reassemble it in a new way as she did with the Cala House was a practical lesson that Zegers took to heart. Her poetic words may originate in Spanish, but they are in the language of sensitivity, which knows no linguistic boundaries. Zegers is a rare combination of self-assurance and fundamental modesty, and this duality is at the heart of her work—she has dared to go in architecture where few women in Chile had been before her; she has dared to speak with her own voice. At first, she encountered opposition to her avant-garde positions, but her newly liberated seventy-six-year-old mother and young people kissing the walls of her chapel made it clear that she had found things that others had set aside or never seen. She had found her voice.

**Philip Jodidio**
Paris, August 2023

# Thesis on Territory

The thesis on territory is an artistic method that shows how an idea materializes in a three-dimensional space.

The process involves crossing through a territory with a poetic word that emerges from the contemplative observation of a scene or simply by chance. As the poet Stéphane Mallarmé said, *Un coup de dés jamais n'abolira le hasard* (*A Roll of the Dice Will Never Abolish Chance*). As a result, the process involves three stages of materialization:

Gesture—Figure—Form

The word *poiesis* comes from the Latin *poeticus* and the Greek *polëtikos*. It refers to how an idea emerges, passing from *not being* to *being* by assuming a name or a title. The *poetic word* thus is defined as the first moment in the existence of a building.

For the fiftieth anniversary celebration of the PUCV (Pontificia Universidad Católica de Valparaíso), the architecture school I attended, each former student was asked to define the synthesis of their practices. Organizing my projects, I realized that I had been conceiving of my process in a different way, starting with Einstein's well-known mass-energy equivalence $E=mc^2$. I created architectural forms starting with the question, how dense is matter? I imagined that architecture is more than a finished project—it is a prototype, where each form can evolve into another.

My work also involves the contemporary language of Latin America, which is related to the vastness of the territory—the last frontiers. Creating architecture in relation to a territory through the medium of a poetic word becomes what has been called *geopoetics*:

Territory is to America what monuments are to Europe

The sounds that emerge from energy are also part of this concept:
1. Opening = energy deployment **Sound**
2. Synthesis = embrace + the condensation of energy **Silence**
3. Balance = deployment + embrace **Harmony**

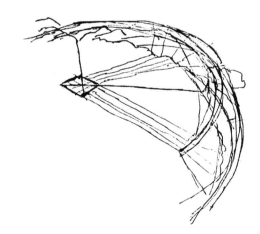

Rhombus square, landscape figure

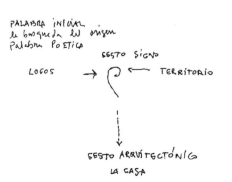

**GEOPOETICS**
POIESES (Greek) - POIESIS (Latin) = to pass from the NOT BEEN to the BEEN

I organized the work into three categories related to sound, which has to do with energy:

**Space is also energy**
$E = mc^2$

|  | Casa Cala | Casa del Agua | Casa del Fuego | Casa Luna | Open Office |
|---|---|---|---|---|---|

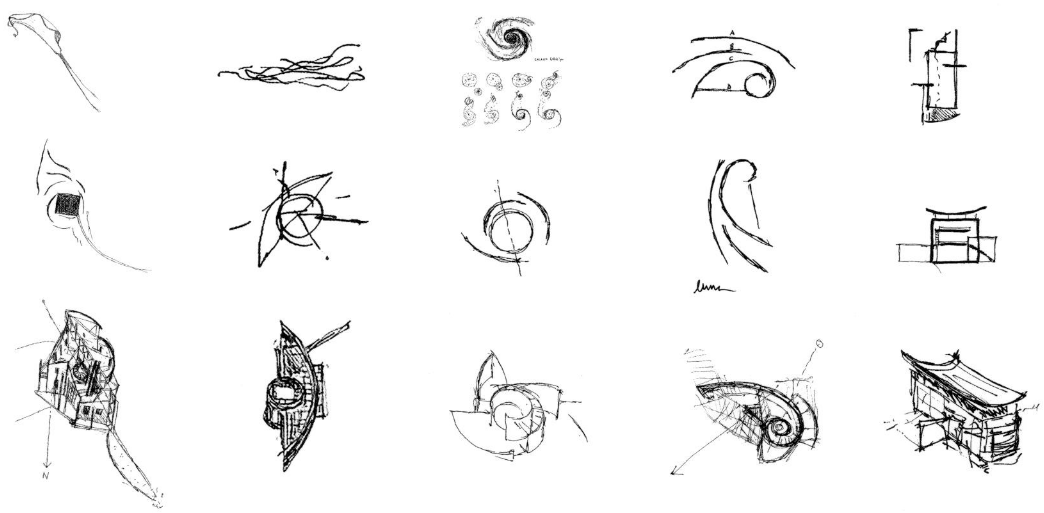

**Opening**
Energy deployment
(Sound)

|  | Casa Granero | Casa Cáscara | Casa Cubo | Casa Do | Casa Haiku |
|---|---|---|---|---|---|

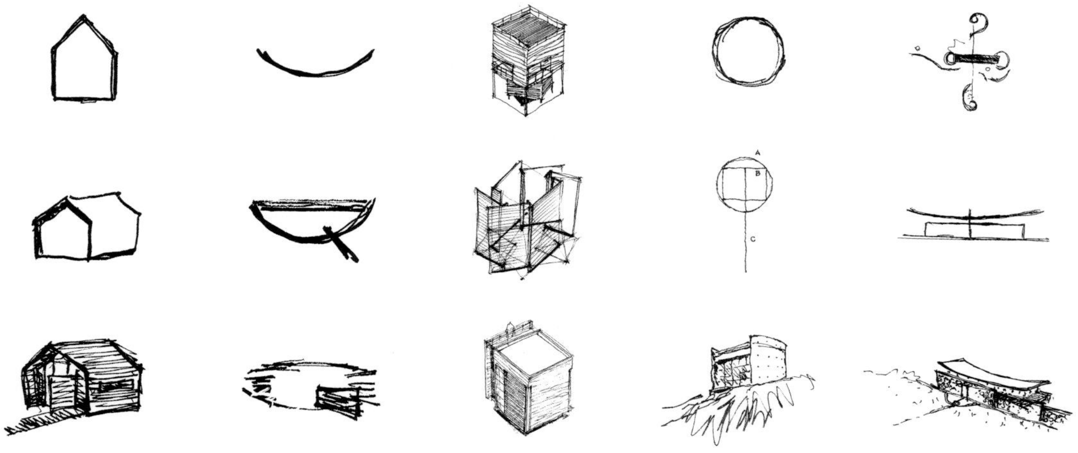

**Synthesis**
Containment and energy condensation
(Silence)

|  | Hotel del Viento | Chilco Lodge | Casa Esmeralda | Capilla Espíritu Santo | Hotel Magnolia |
|---|---|---|---|---|---|

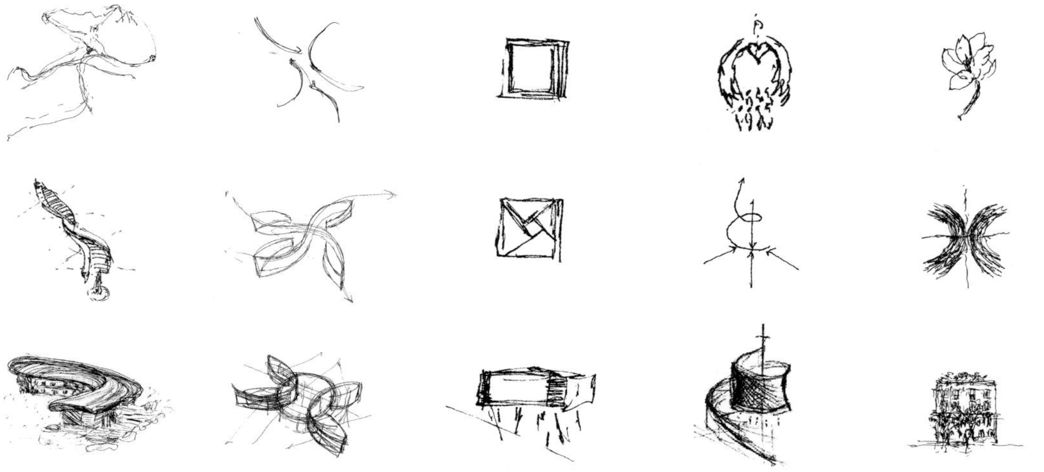

**Balance**
Deployment and containment are in balance
(Harmony)

# I.

# Concrete

Capilla Holy Spirit
Espíritu Chapel
Santo
Casa
Do Do House
Casa
Breath House Soplo

# Capilla Espíritu Santo

Holy Spirit
Chapel

La palabra poética dice:
Abrazo
de Dios padre a su comunidad
deambular envolver, ascender
conexión espiritual
Silencio

The poetic word says:
Embrace of God the father of his community.
Wander around, surround, ascend. Spiritual connection. Silence.

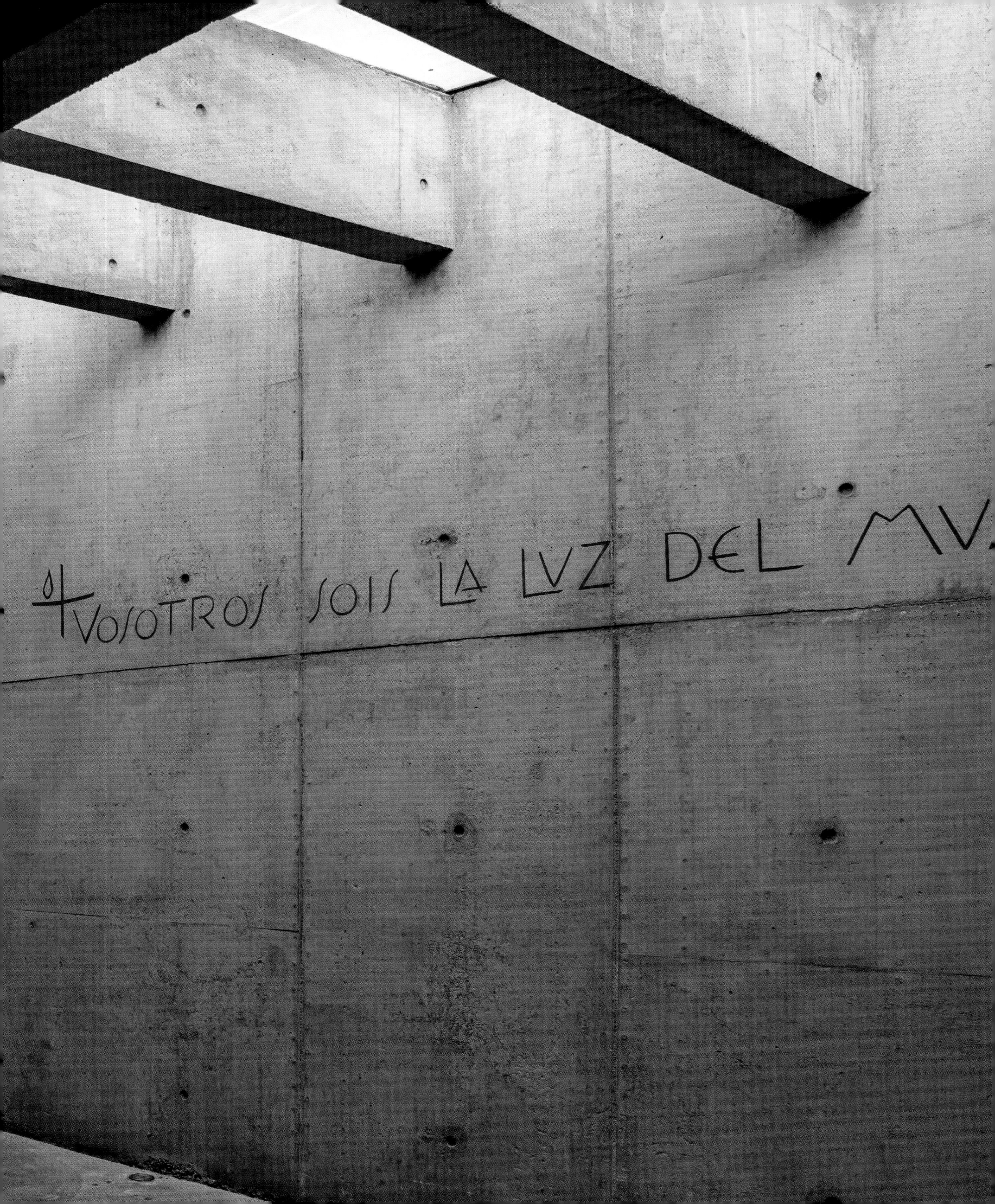
VOSOTROS SOIS LA LUZ DEL MU

Casa
Do

*La palabra poética dice*

*Do*

*antiguo Ut*

*Útero habitable frente al Pacífico*

02

The poetic word says:
Do. Ancient Ut.
Habitable womb facing the Pacific.

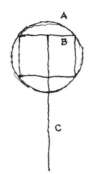

# Casa Soplo

Breath House

*La palabra poética dice*
*Soplo.*
*"lo que insufla la vida a la materia inerente"*
*fibonacci*
*plataforma de despegue al paisaje*

The poetic word says:
Breath. What breathes life into matter. *Fibonacci.*
Take-off platform to the landscape.

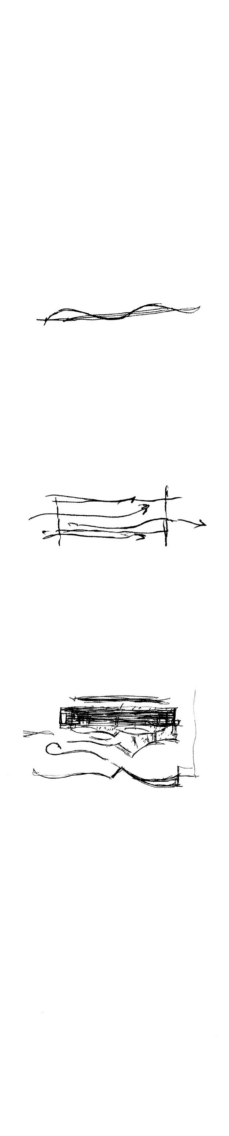

CONCRETE

# II.
# Timber

Casa
Esme-
ralda Emerald House
Casa
Ye Ye House
Casa
Lum House Lum

# Casa
# Esme-
# ralda

Emerald House

04

The poetic word says:
Emerald. Fractal crystal, Platonic polyhedra. Icosahedron.
Void rotating to the contemporary.

# Casa Ye

Ye House

*La palabra poética dice*
*Ye*
*síntesis abstracta habitable*
*alfabeto de formas*

The poetic word says:
Ye. Habitable abstract synthesis.
Alphabet of forms.

Casa
Lum

La palabra poética dice
LUM
La Última Morada
pabellón en diálogo
con el jardín

The poetic word says:
Lum. The last dwelling.
Pavilion in dialogue with the garden.

# III.
# Hospitality

Tierra
Pata-
gonia

Tierra Patagonia Hotel

Mag-
nolia

Magnolia Hotel

Casa
Llu

Llu House Family Lodge

House of Fire
Family Lodge

Casa
del Fuego

Casa
Pyr

Pyr House
Family Lodge

# Tierra Pata-gonia

Tierra Patagonia
Hotel

La palabra poética
dice
Viento
el territorio dice hombre en libertad
sobre el territorio
formas que dibuja el viento = fuselaje

The poetic word says:
Wind. The territory says: man in freedom over the territory.
Forms drawn by wind = fuselage.

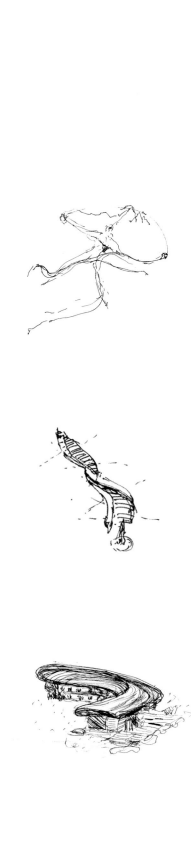

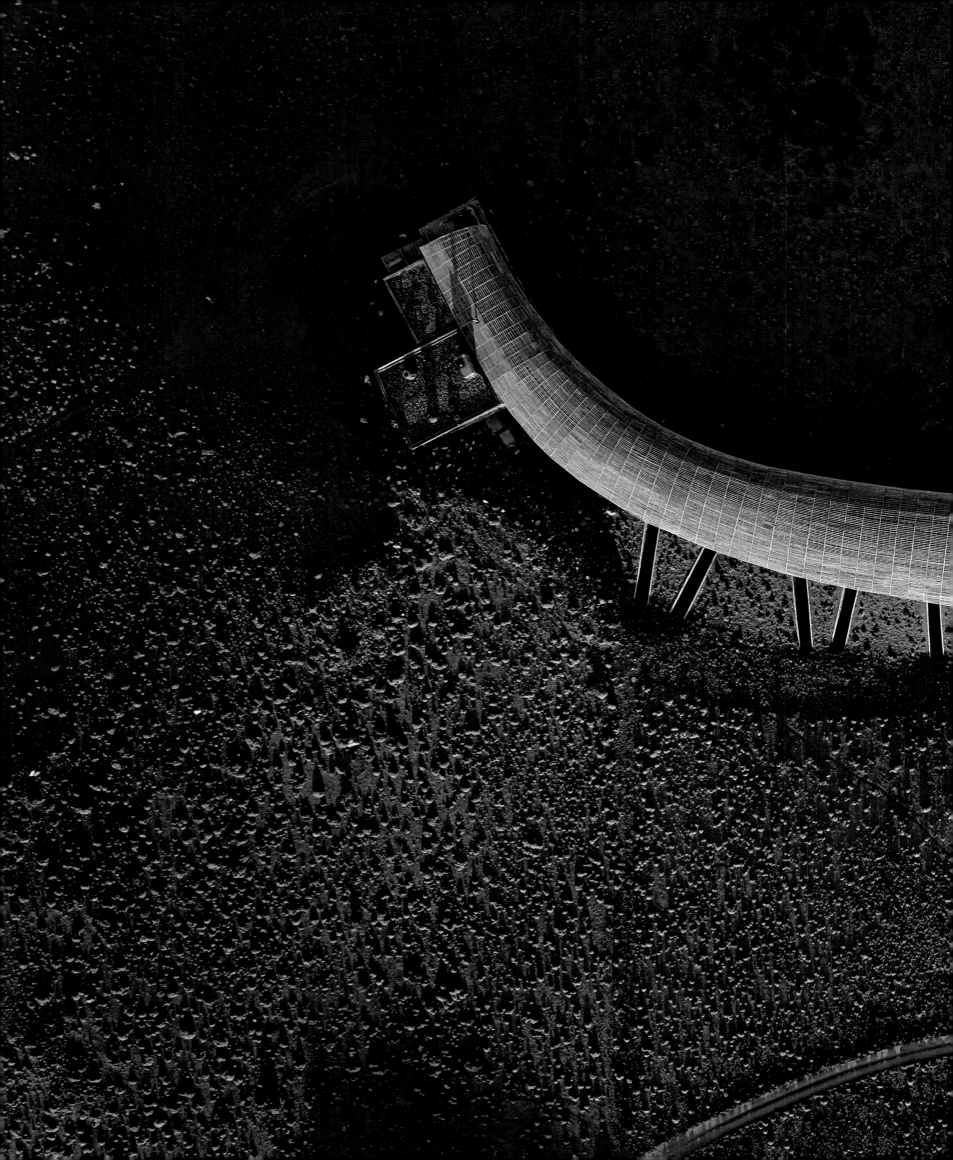

# Mag-nolia

Magnolia
Hotel

La palabra poética dice
Magnolia
resonancia de lo antiguo con lo nuevo
Reflejo
desapareciente y Líquido.

The poetic word says:
Magnolia. Resonance of the old with the new.
Reflection, vanishing, and liquid.

MAGNOLIA    HOTEL

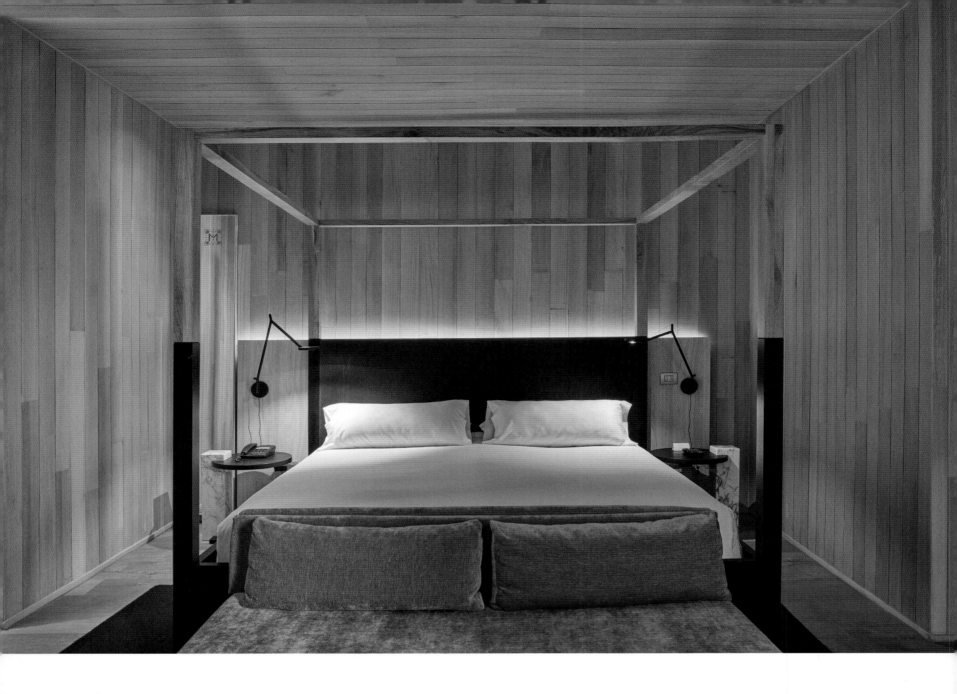

# Casa Llu

Llu House
Family Lodge

*La palabra poética dice
Lluvia
manto para la Lluvia
H2O = Llu*

The poetic word says:
Rain. Cloak for the rain.
$H_2O$ = Llu.

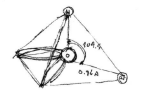

# Casa del Fuego

House of Fire
Family Lodge

La palabra poética dice

Fuego
de las erupciones volcanicas
que dan forma a un Territorio
Leve
Fuego Leve
Galaxia Espiral

The poetic word says:
Fire from the volcanic eruptions that give shape to a territory. Mild.
Mild fire = Spiral Galaxy.

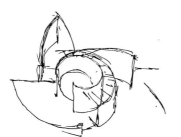

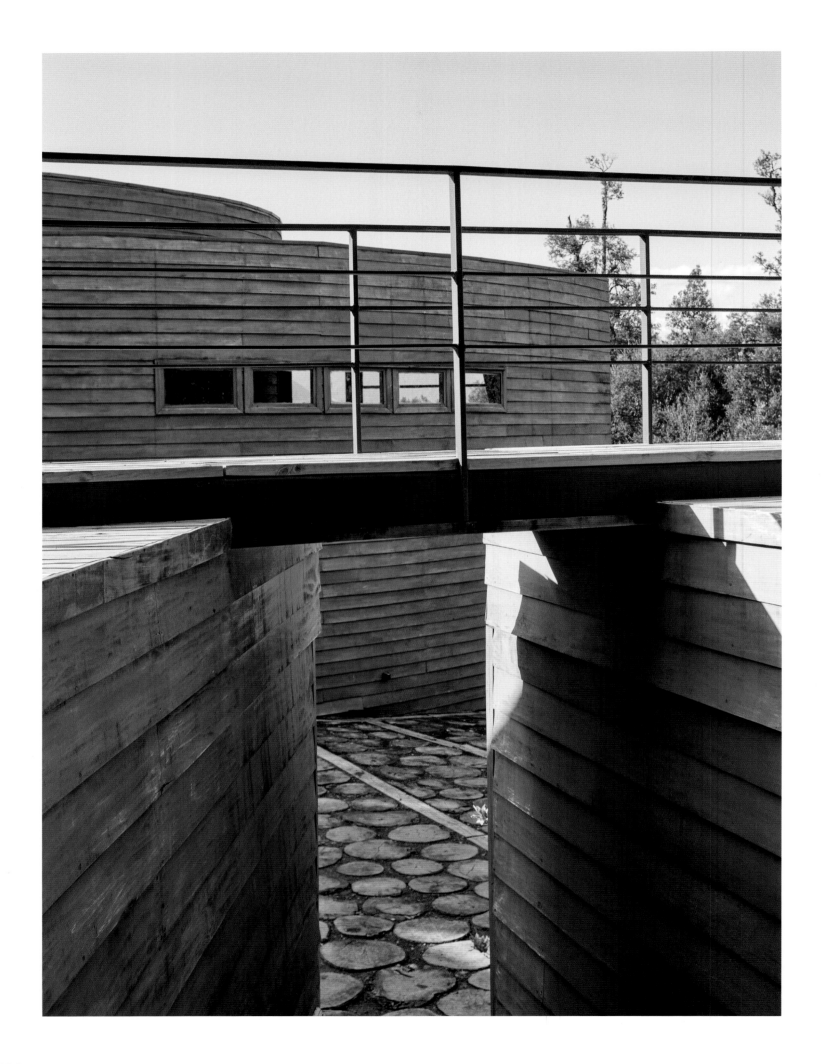

# Casa Pyr

Pyr House
Family Lodge

La palabra poética dice

Pyrita = Pyr

piedra del hogar, = fuego del hogar

geometría Sagrada .

del fuego

The poetic word says:
Pyrite = Pyr. Home stone = Home fire.
Sacred geometry of fire.

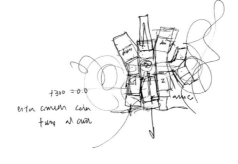

# IV.
# Tiny Projects

# Pueblo <small>Tiny House</small>

# Pueblo

Tiny House

La palabra poética dice
        Pueblo = Timidez Botánica
los árboles dejan callejuelas entre sí
    El follaje son Pixeles en el territorio.

The poetic word says:
Town = Botanical shyness. The trees leave alleys between each other.
Foliage takes the form of pixels in the territory.

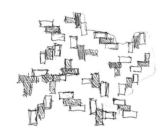

# V. Geopoetics

The territory is to America
what monuments are to Europe

# "The Territory is to America what Monuments are to Europe"

In 1943, the Uruguayan writer and artist Joaquín Torres-García imagined an inversion of power between what is North and South in America, creating his famous drawing of an inverted American continent. This idea was reexamined in 1965 when a collective of poets, artists, and architects quoted Torres-García when he said: "Our North is our South . . . The tip of America, from now on, extending, insistently points to the South, our North" (Torres-García, 1944, *La Escuela del Sur*). The collective followed this idea and wrote an epic poem titled *Amereida*, declaring that "Amereida is the combination of Virgil's *Aeneid* with America, as a way to re-create and determine our continent within a poetic vision." The Mexican historian and philosopher Edmundo O'Gorman (1906–1995) had a theory which argued that Columbus was searching for the Indies and did not realize that he had arrived on a new continent. In *Amereida*: "America emerges as a gift—a donation, a Latin American culture that must be created." Based on these ideas, my process has long examined the question of what constitutes an original work. I think that Latin America has something to say to the world, and this is about a way of doing and thinking with what "we have on hand"; this is a Low Tech posture. It is an attitude that learns from local processes and techniques and imagines a way to inhabit, leaving traces across a territory. It proposes a new culture, which will emerge when we, the people of Latin America, understand that the way to relate to this land is in a "light and precarious way." This attitude of respect and balance learns from the practices of the original cultures of this territory—a *métissage* of the blood and cultural forms of the aboriginals (originals) and the conquerors. Between the earthen rites of the originals and the Christian rites of the conquerors who came from Europe, there is a third way that I call the Astral Being. The Astral Being is a mediator between two energies: the Dionysiac, sensual and spontaneous, and the Apol-lonian, rational, ordered, and self-disciplined with a capacity for abstraction. And from this combination a new culture might come forth. To achieve this result, we must build "signs" in the territory, the starting points of a contemporary cultural landscape.

## Threshold Plazas

These Architectural Signs could inaugurate a place and open the land to new narratives. In 2017, I cocreated the Andes Workshop with Grupo Talca, a collaborative and interdisciplinary educational platform dedicated to designing and building these signs in multiple and diverse territories. In 2017, we created the Patachoique Threshold Plaza with six students worldwide, some collaborators from the local Indigenous Pehuenche community, and Pedro Vasquez, a carpenter. Located in the Andean region of Araucanía, the Ruta Pehuenche is a hiking and cultural path, conceived around the territory's five volcanoes (Tolhuaca, Lonquimay, Sierra Nevada, Llaima, and Nevados de Sollipulli). Today this Threshold Plaza is recognized by Ladera Sur as one of the five thresholds to visit in Chile. In 2018, we built the Plazoleta Negra Threshold Plaza, located in the Central Chilean Andes, with a student, the local community, and collaborators. We also opened the Santiago Outdoor Capital of Latin America project. The center of this scheme is the reflection of Latin America's capital cities, which grow chaotically, creating various forms of asymmetry. The project proposes to understand the city of Santiago, beginning with its natural environment and the opportunity this offers residents to connect with nature, fresh air, and freedom. Today we are working on a Patrimonial Route from the Plaza de Armas—Santiago's main square—to the highest mountain peak visible from the city, the Cerro El Plomo (5,434 meters).

**VOLCANOES OF THE ARAUCANÍA ANDEAN NORTH**

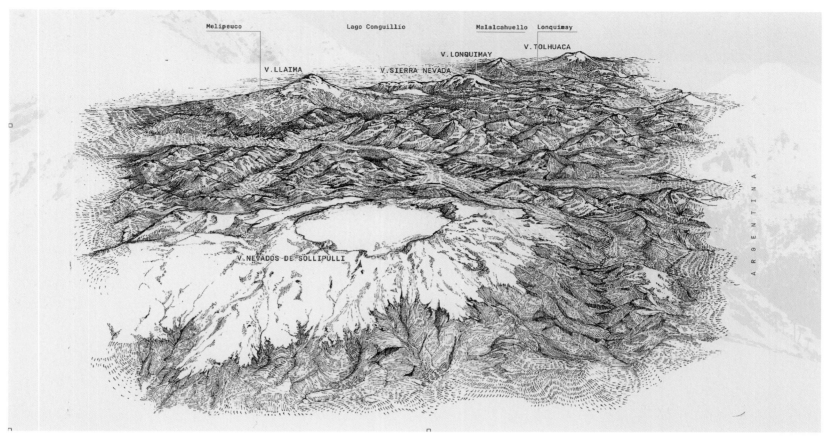

Illustration by José Domingo Hernández

**PLAZOLETA PATACHOIQUE THRESHOLD VIEWPOINT LOCATED IN LONQUIMAY**

Photo by Rodrigo Sheward

"THE TERRITORY IS TO AMERICA WHAT MONUMENTS ARE TO EUROPE"

Photo by Os Espacialistas

*What happened to poetry in the digital age?*
*What is happening to the social body? To space as an*
*expression of poetic*
*language? What are the limits of a language and the limits*
*of the*
*world? Poetry as excess.*
*A* Threshold *is an installation that connects directly with*
*internal and external journeys . . .*

This threshold, understood as a gesture in space, is about how a person and matter operate in the three-dimensional space, where the y-axis is an evocation of "becoming" governed by temporality. We come from a certain past with our traditions, an apacheta (ancestral stone monolith to show the way) leading the way to enter the threshold. The z-axis appears as the eternal present, tying us to the land and connecting us with spirituality. The x-axis appears to be the balance of oppositions—feminine-masculine, dark-light, night-day, and so forth. I think that only from this awareness can we open new futures with novel possibilities, seeking to rebalance the world. Perhaps, then, we won't be the next species to disappear from the planet.

**Manifest**
Ko_yaa_nis_qatsil (in Hopi language)
(1) crazy life, (2) life in turmoil, (3) life out of balance, (4) life that is disintegrating, (5) a state of life that calls for another way of living

In his 1982 experimental documentary, *Koyaanisqatsi: Life Out of Balance* (the first part of the *Qatsi* trilogy), American film director Godfrey Reggio calls attention to what is happening today to the relationships among human beings, nature, and technology. I understand this meaning in evolution as the premonition of the process that mankind is facing. The 1980s were crazy life; the 1990s were life in turmoil; the 2000s were life out of balance; the 2010s, life disintegrating; and today is a state of life that calls for another way of living. The demands on architects now are enormous, because architecture must reflect on these matters and confront the challenge of the new paradigm that is emerging with the rise of a new culture. This is a culture that I like to describe as the "American" or the "Pacifican." This word game suggests that America and the Pacific offer clues to a response, mainly because in these territories, there are original aboriginal cultures with languages and visions of the cosmos that reconnect the human being to the land, as a living part of its complex ecosystem, but at the same time as ritual beings, not the dominators seen through established religions. We must return to the land and its original balance—understand it as sacred. If we don't do so, the human species will disappear from the planet. The human species belongs to the earth; we cannot develop life separate from her, because we are part of the land in an intimately connected process. We face the urgency of reconnecting to new, open forms and achieving more sustainable ways of life. In a postindustrial era, our development cannot be based on extractive models but on collaborative and circular methods. The role of architecture today is to open new narratives about the territory that will allow us to build healthy cities, balancing life in a post-technological world. This paradigm change is necessarily accompanied by rebalancing the feminine energy of the being and Indigenous communities in the cultural process. It is necessary to recover our connection to nature and the sacred ancestral ways so that we can pass from an egocentric society to an ecocentric society.

We are also working on the Threshold Plaza AMA, located at the north entry of Santiago's Metropolitan Park. This territorial sign opens with the "Museo Abierto," a women's museum for the 21st century. This idea started in my spring advanced design studio at Yale (2020), where my students attended and experienced the Andes Workshop in Chile and proposed eleven ideas for the future museum, most of them arising from the social needs of the community after the 2019 Chilean social crisis. AMA is the Ancestral Women's Agora, a place to debate citizens' differences, and to find common ground on different views. This threshold appeared in a recent art exhibition at Galería Gallo, in Santiago de Chile, curated by Patricio Pozo, where I gave form in space to the concept of the future "Museo Abierto."

I like to call myself an AMA: Artist, Mujer (Woman), Architect. This is also a play on the term *ama de casa* (housewife) or *amante* (lover), to speak about my work, which is based on the love affair between a building and a territory, or the love for the community. The purpose of my work is the love for Mother Earth, which sustains all life.

As Patricio Pozo wrote in a curatorial text in Santiago in 2023:

> *In Platonism, poetry prohibits discursive thinking: dianoia,*
> *which is the result of discursive thinking. The poem exists*
> *on the threshold. It is not a crossing point subject to rules,*
> *but rather an offering, a proposal without rules.*

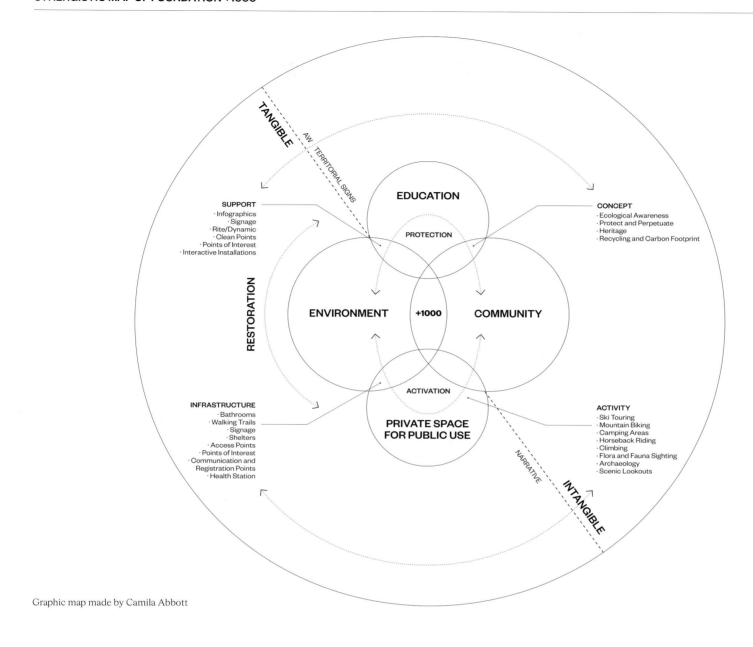

TANGIBLE

AW. TERRITORIAL SIGNS

**SUPPORT**
· Infographics
· Signage
· Rite/Dynamic
· Clean Points
· Points of Interest
· Interactive Installations

**CONCEPT**
· Ecological Awareness
· Protect and Perpetuate
· Heritage
· Recycling and Carbon Footprint

RESTORATION

**EDUCATION**

PROTECTION

**ENVIRONMENT**   **+1000**   **COMMUNITY**

ACTIVATION

**PRIVATE SPACE
FOR PUBLIC USE**

**INFRASTRUCTURE**
· Bathrooms
· Walking Trails
· Signage
· Shelters
· Access Points
· Points of Interest
· Communication and
  Registration Points
· Health Station

**ACTIVITY**
· Ski Touring
· Mountain Biking
· Camping Areas
· Horseback Riding
· Climbing
· Flora and Fauna Sighting
· Archaeology
· Scenic Lookouts

NARRATIVE

INTANGIBLE

Graphic map made by Camila Abbott

Photo Lee Busel

"THE TERRITORY IS TO AMERICA WHAT MONUMENTS ARE TO EUROPE"

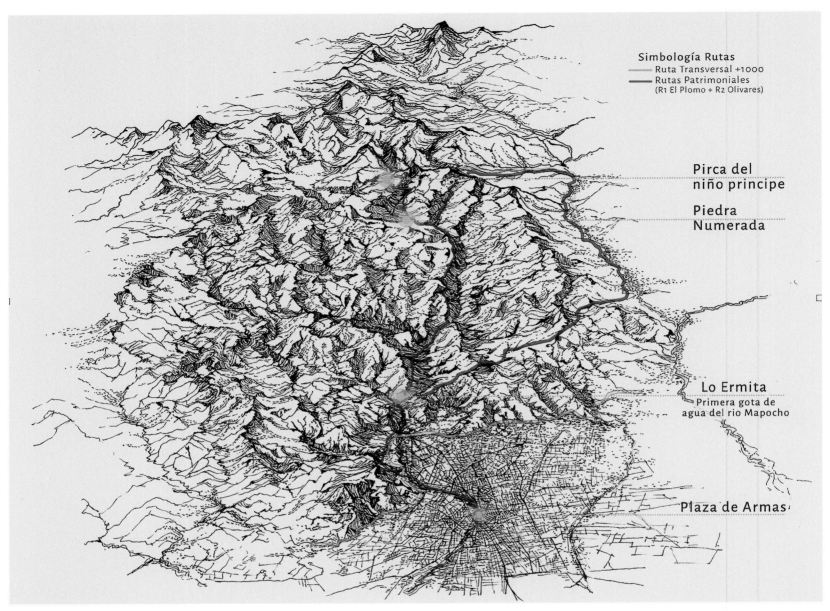

Simbología Rutas
Ruta Transversal +1000
Rutas Patrimoniales
(R1 El Plomo + R2 Olivares)

Pirca del
niño principe

Piedra
Numerada

Lo Ermita
Primera gota de
agua del rio Mapocho

Plaza de Armas

Illustration by José Domingo Hernández

**Words from the Andes Workshop teachers:**

The emphasis is on the person, in relation to a volcano and a territory, and not on things.

**Rodrigo Sheward**
Architect/Grupo Talca

In my case, this is an opportunity to think intuitively about graphic solutions for architectural problems.

**Teresa Montero**
Designer

The work with Andes Workshop has been vital for my work; this bio-geo-poetic inhabiting of the territory has a sensitive form. Interdisciplinary work with the other professions is vital today, staying on the edge and listening.

**Sergio Elortegui**
Naturalist

The first experience of the Andes Workshop has marked a starting point in the way of understanding the processes. It allowed me to understand the un-limits, the relationships I could establish with dance, and with other areas, opening up to different dimensions, to other visualities—sound, and other modes of production proposing new aesthetic twists.

**Francisca Sazie**
Choreographer

Through different actions, with a strong emphasis on formative and educational experiences, Andes Workshop was established as an expanded and experimental field, where it is possible to reimagine a future for our planet.

**Cristián Silva-Avária**
Visual Artist

Photo Lee Busel

It's about having a connection to matter. My participation as a sculptor in the Andes Workshop Plazoleta Negra Threshold was stimulating. Today Umbral Plazoleta Negra is a meeting place, of silence and contemplation. That is the collective sense of what we are doing. By building these places with the local communities, in different landscapes of our territory, we are rediscovering nature, sensitizing and making ourselves aware of it at the same time.

**Vicente Gajardo**
Sculptor

A space where time is not measured in hours but by flexible and innovative shared experiences. This calls for reflection, enriched by the multidisciplinary nature of those who make up this group.

**Jessica Torres**
Sculptor

After tracing, cutting, and talking about assemblies, we walk back through the woods, happy and satisfied, celebrating a productive day of work and learning.

**Héctor Ducci**
Architect/Vernacular Carpenter

In general, architects can, from their spatial experience, open the senses to words, to move through them like the images and materials that shelter us.

**Claudio Valdés Mujica**
Poet

We have enjoyed the co-creation of poetic experiences—milestones for the transformation of the consciousness of our students, so that they can contribute as agents of change.

**Aleka Vial**
Journalist

# VI.
# Projects
# Technical
# Details

# Capilla Espíritu Santo

Holy Spirit Chapel
2003

**Location:**
Puente Alto
Metropolitan Region, Santiago, Chile

**Collaborators:**
Loreto Tolosa
Roger Tuhoy
Francisco García Huidobro

**Structural Engineering:**
VPA
Enzo Valladares

**Lighting Design:**
Joyce Lowstein

**Mural:**
Claudio Pastor

**Stained Glass:**
Pilar Argandoña

**Furniture Design:**
Denisse Lizama

**Wall Calligraphy:**
Teresa Montero

**Landscape:**
Adriana Valdés

This church in a poor peripheral neighborhood of Santiago had the potential to be of great significance for the local community. If done right, the building could become a source of social transformation.

With this in mind, and our being new to the subject, our first questions were about how a church should be designed. What is the source of its form and what might be the role of what some people call *divine coincidence*? Around the same time, a young theologian came to the office to ask us to design her house. She told us: "The church is the form of the community."

As it happens, the community proved to be happy, supportive, and hardworking. They imagined a round space, where the altar is close to the people, with wide corridors to meet and talk. This church would not look like a small house but have the true scale of a temple.

The architectural gesture that defines the church seeks to lead, envelop, and connect with the divine. The shape is generated by a single wall that wraps around the space without closing in on itself. It is open to the light, like the hands of God lovingly welcoming His community. Two voids define the church: the interior space of prayer and the open void of the atrium, where meetings take place. These voids are linked by a route that begins at the base of the bell tower and rises to the maximum height of the church, where a dialogue takes place, in a connecting flow of different orders of magnitude.

The atrium evokes the geographic significance of the Andean landscape, but also that of the divine. It develops the vertical dimension in the urban space, within a context of low and homogeneous buildings. At the same time, the height of the bell tower makes the church a landmark within the neighborhood, observable from a distance. The assembly, the interior void where the rites of Mass take place, is a serene, silent, and centered space. These spatial elements flow according to the "centrifugal force" of the route of the faithful, giving rise to a density that embraces the ceremonies of the Catholic church.

The church was developed from a single gesture that rises and peels back to accommodate the parts of the program—the same one investigated years ago at the Cala House, with another project scale. This time the gesture goes from the ground to the sky to connect with the divine. And contrary to the house, the ascending gesture opens to the central skylight and what we call the light of Christ. Likewise, the walls are expanded through the use of a slit of light, again an analogy to the hands of God the Father welcoming his community.

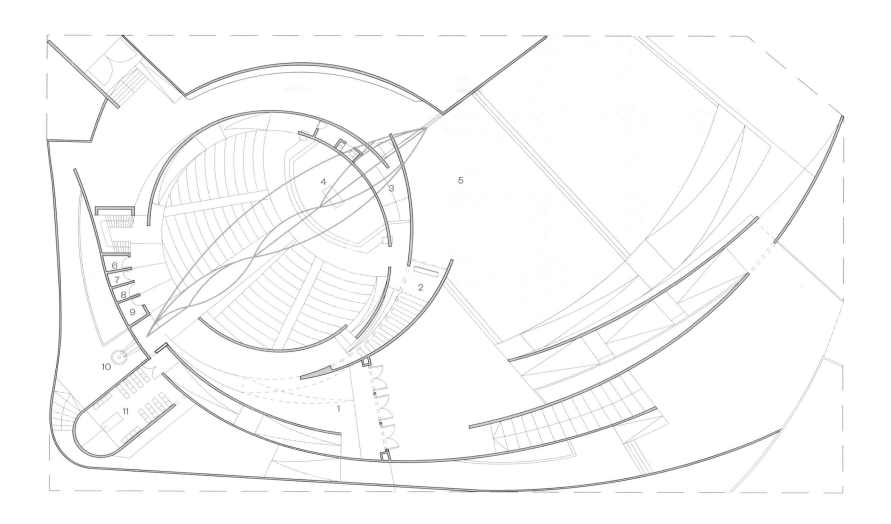

▲ **First Level Plan**
1. Access / 2. Chapel / 3. Sacristy / 4. Altar /
5. Exterior Altar / 6. Closed Confessional / 7. Father's
Room / 8. Open Confessional / 9. Locutory /
10. Flower Pergola / 11. Wake Chapel

◄ **Original Sketch by Cazú Zegers**

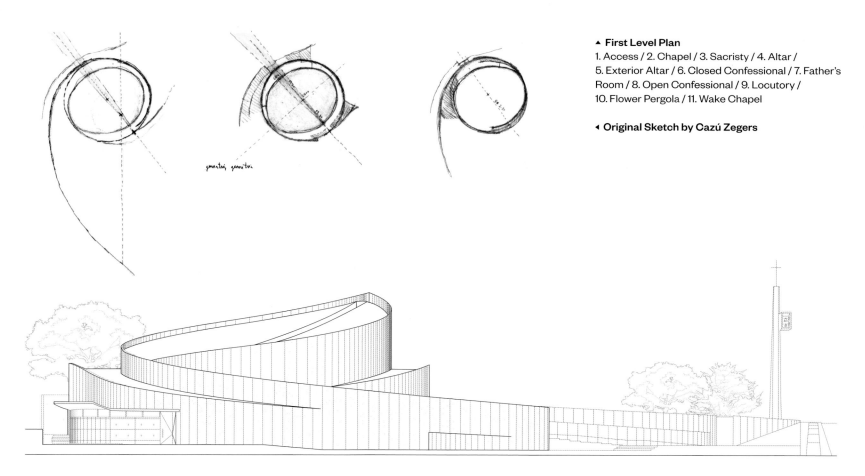

▲ **Elevation**

# Casa Do

Do House
2000

**Location:**
Los Vilos
Coquimbo Region, Chile

**Collaborators:**
Juan Pablo Almarza
Pamela Liddle

**Structural Engineering:**
OPH
Óscar Paredes

**Furniture Design:**
María Luisa Zegers

**Landscape:**
Francisca Vial

This commission involved a house for weekend and vacation use, located in a family condominium complex with other existing structures. The design is based on the imperative to generate a matrix, a womb of protection against the vastness of the sea, which allows for contemplation within a temperate interior. The *I Ching* refers to the image of a well, suggesting that going further within produces greater clarity.

The architectural process in this instance is one of subtraction. We decided to build a concrete circle, precisely like a well. The architectural gesture is a circle, crossed by a line, which denotes access to the house and the division of public space from private. The complexity of spatial resolution lies in the intersection of two orders: the enveloping circular versus orthogonal regularity. The circle dialogues with the external environment in a synthetic way—not constructing a new typology but referring instead to the iconic image of a pool of water.

The architectural operation circumscribes a rectangle within the circle, generating a relationship of solids and voids to the parent circle. The empty ones to the east and west are used to open windows, and the full ones, two sizable, curved side walls, form arcs that support slabs, creating three levels of living space.

The meeting of the rectangle with the curved walls forms a dilation that becomes a source of overhead light. Joinery is used in objects and furniture, which are incorporated to articulate the public and private programs. Leading up to the roof terrace, a handmade laminated wooden staircase forms a sculptural object within the space.

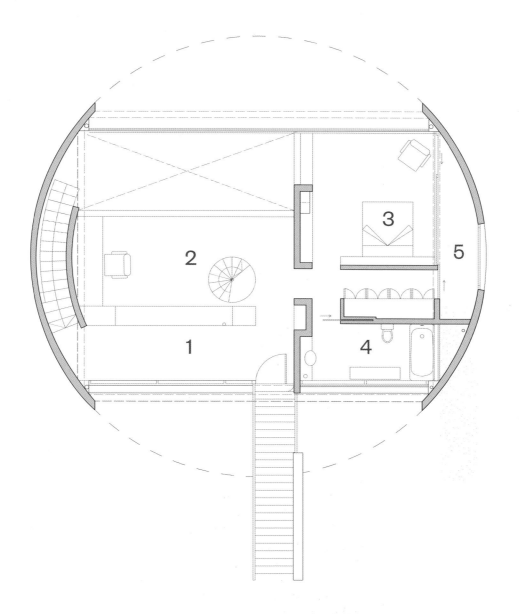

▲ **First Level Plan**
1. Access / 2. Desk / 3. Bedroom / 4. Bathroom / 5. Garden

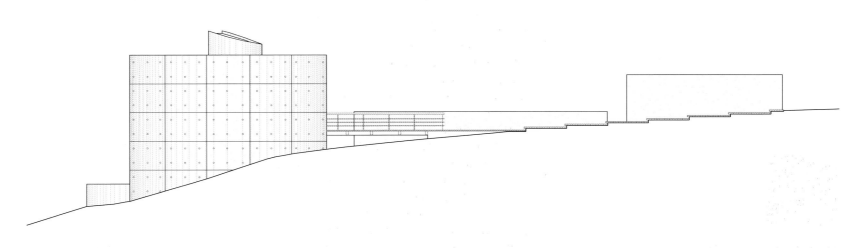

▲ **South Elevation**

# Casa Soplo

Breath House
2011

**Location:**
Lo Barnechea
Metropolitan Region, Santiago de Chile, Chile

**Collaborators:**
Francisco García Huidobro

**Structural Engineering:**
OPH
Óscar Paredes

**Lighting Design:**
Diseño de LUZ
Paulina Sir
Gaspar Arenas

**Sculpture Elements:**
Jessica Torres

**Landscape:**
Teresa Moller

**Short Documentary Film:**
Pablo Cassals

*Soplo*, meaning "to breathe" or "to blow" in English, is what gives life to inert matter.

It is the wind that gently passes and leaves its trace on sand or snow. This house, located in an extraordinary urban space, was planned as a "continuous pavilion open to the landscape."

The west facade, which coincides with the entrance, appears to be hermetically closed by curved walls. This design was inspired by a visit to the Guggenheim Bilbao with my fifteen-year-old daughter Clara. She felt strong emotions upon seeing the curving Corten steel sculptures of Richard Serra exhibited there. I said to myself: "If someday I design my own house, I want to create the same experience or emotion as the sculptures of Richard Serra."

So when the time came, the house resolved these curved spaces with a double system related to the golden ratio, and to the study of the shapes carved out by a soft wind over sand and snow, giving form to the idea of breath.

This home, located in the foothills of the Cerro Manquehue, was created to liberate the "feminine aspects of the being." The intention was not to produce a unique, or different, architecture but to instead generate a homogeneous facade with the neighboring house (that of my sister), designed by the architect Luis Izquierdo. Thus, the house assumes the lines of the earlier Rollán Zegers house by Izquierdo, opening a vast territory to the eye. I did not want to create an "ego-unique" architectural object, but instead a very discrete one, related to the landscape and allowing for a warm and temperate residence.

The interior was imagined through a process of extreme subtraction, where the Andean landscape serves as the protagonist of space. This is achieved by using a large transparent facade, open to the views, which allows the space to be entirely connected. As a unique, flexible, or democratic space, it allows for different uses. A second, hermetic circulation space is located at the back, where the curved walls define the perimeter. Skylights are generated where the curves meet the main line of the space, allowing light into this rear circulation zone.

In Casa Soplo, living occurs in a continuous flow, between interior and exterior, horizontally and vertically. This dynamic volume, without imposed spatial hierarchies, allows the 15,000-sq. ft. (1,400-m²) site to seem infinite, with endless possibilities.

The roof is proposed as a fifth facade. Covered with a timber viewing deck and flowers, this space contributes to the thermal efficiency of the house. The garden concept is that of an "urban farm," inspired by agricultural landscaping, planted in a system of curved terraces that follow a dialogue with the access walls, flanked by a 82-foot (25-meter)-long swimming pool that adds an abstract line of water to the landscape and the garden.

The interior design was conceived with sculptural wooden elements such as a stairway that offers an inner connection from the garden to the roof. The sculptor Jessica Torres created the hangers and door handles. The intention is to achieve a meeting and dialogue between architecture and sculpture.

For me, the simple complexity of Casa Soplo offers a reflection on contemporary living and is a prototype that opens a new path for architecture. Referring back to Emerald House (Santiago, 2014), my mother's home, I developed similar ideas in a more consistent way in the Casa Soplo.

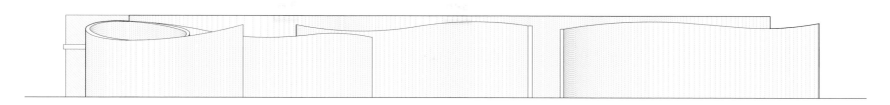

▲ South Elevation

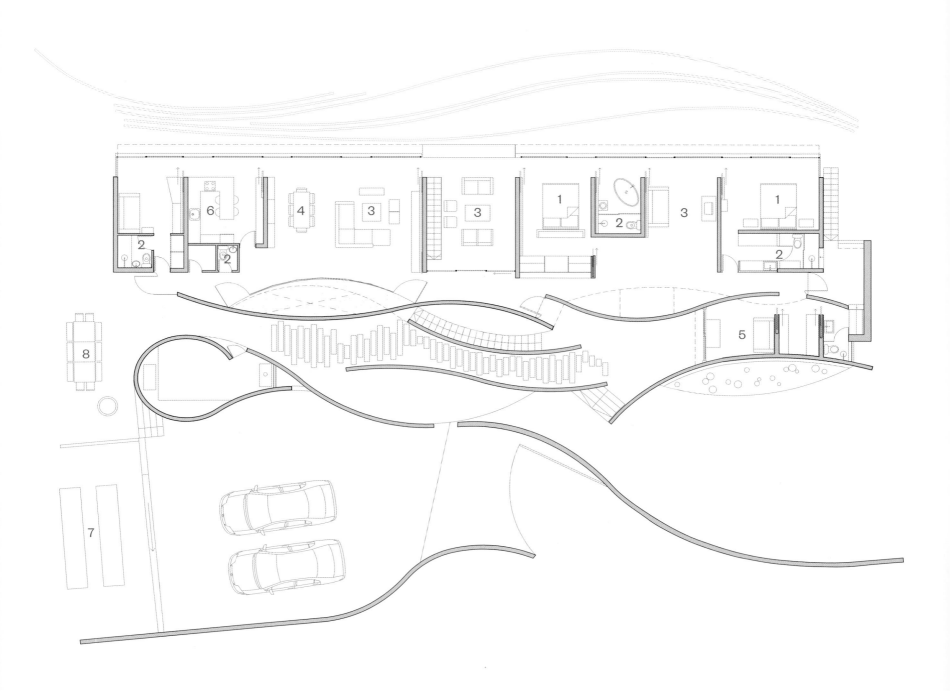

▲ First Level Plan

1. Bedroom / 2. Bathroom / 3. Living Room / 4. Dining Room / 5. Workshop / 6. Kitchen / 7. Garden / 8. Barbecue Area

# Casa Esmeralda

Emerald House
2014

**Location:**
Lo Barnechea
Metropolitan Region, Santiago, Chile

**Associated Architects:**
Ian Hsü
Gabriel Rudolphy

**Collaborators:**
Yolanda Muñoz

**Structural Engineering:**
VPA
Enzo Valladares

**Lighting Design:**
Diseño de LUZ
Paulina Sir
Gaspar Arenas

**Decoration:**
María Luisa Zegers

**Landscape:**
Teresa Moller

**Short Documentary Film:**
Pablo Cassals

Inspired by the traditional Roman house with its central impluvium, this construction has a regular square plan, with a central courtyard—a void around which the interior circulation is created. This configuration also provides light and passive ventilation to the residence.

The poetic word *esmeralda* comes from the eye color of the owner, a rare and beautiful green. To develop the design, we studied how an emerald crystal grows in geometric Platonic polyhedra patterns, evolving in complexity up to the icosahedron. This geometric pattern shapes the roof of the house and becomes the main architectonic element of the volume, rotating the center courtyard, with the roof understood as the fifth facade of the residence. The roof of the home which is located in the foothills of the Cerro Manquehue, one of the most prominent points of Santiago, expands its living area. The volume is suspended over a "forest" of concrete columns, allowing the landscape to pass freely under the house, offering a generous intermediate area beneath, used for family gatherings or special occasions. The owner of the house has a large family, so the possibility of the space being either intimate or expanded to hold up to forty-five people was a central issue for the architectural decisions based on the owner's way of living.

The building consists of a wooden fuselage that rises from the ground through inclined concrete pillars representing the image of a "forest," and creating a protected outdoor space from which to look toward the mountain. The open volume beneath the structure fulfills a double function. The entire site becomes a garden, generating a series of intermediate areas that allow inhabitants to enjoy extraordinary views, covered terraces, and a barbecue space for family. And on the other hand, it allows residents to inhabit the exterior of the house almost all year-round, enjoying a mild Mediterranean climate, characteristic of the central part of Chile.

The main space is conceived as a pavilion that opens out to the landscape, with a double circulation around the internal and external perimeters created by the interior patio. The circulation space in front of the vertical facade of the house passes next to the windows without touching them, generating continuity between the different rooms. In this way, we created a flexible space, without hierarchies that restrict their living environment.

In the house, living flows between the interior and the exterior, permitting views of the landscape to extend to the infinite. In its purest state, this structure is an elemental form that creates a dialogue with the territory and with the experience of those who inhabit the house. The emotion of inhabiting a Platonic polyhedron touches on metaphysics and creates a dialogue with the sensitive being.

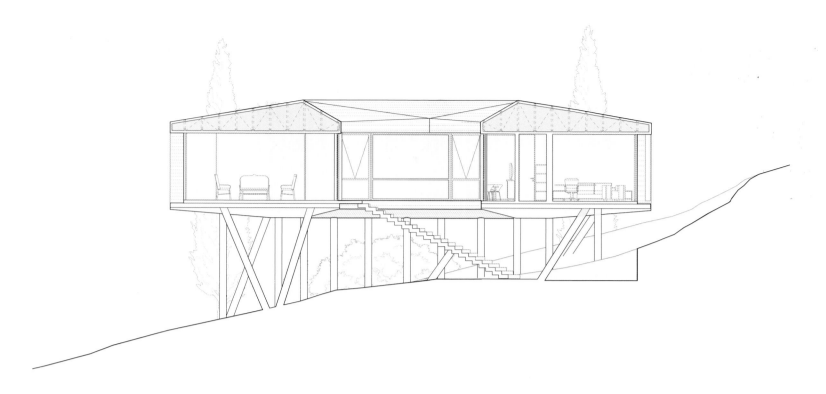

▲ **Cut**

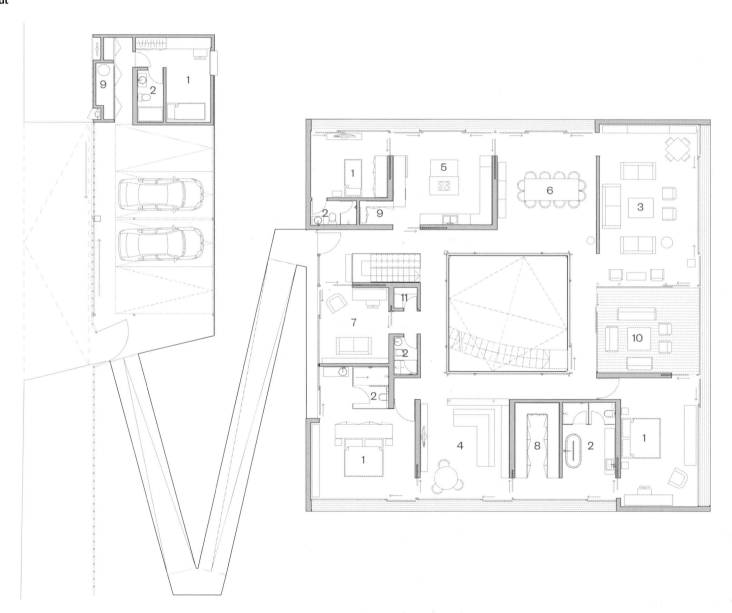

▲ **First Level Plan**

1. Bedroom / 2. Bathroom / 3. Living Room / 4. TV Room / 5. Kitchen / 6. Dining Room / 7. Desk / 8. Closet / 9. Cellar / 10. Terrace / 11. Alarm

# Casa Ye

Ye House
2018

**Location:**
Valdivia
Los Ríos Region, Chile

**Associated Architects:**
Ian Hsü
Gabriel Rudolphy

**Structural Engineering:**
José Manuel Morales

**Lighting Design:**
DIAV
Paulina Villalobos

**Short Documentary Film:**
Clara Films
Producer: Clara Larraín
Director: Shawn Garry

The Ye* House is a pavilion suspended over a landscape of myrtle trees with a privileged view of the Cayumapu River and its wetlands, created after the 1960 earthquake in Valdivia. These wetlands are rich in flora and fauna, including the endemic black-necked swan and a dense layer of vegetation made up of reeds and lotus flowers, among other species characteristic of this area.

The program was for a weekend house for a remarried couple, each with their own family including adult children. Our architectural response consisted of three volumes in the shape of the letter Y. The entrance frames the landscape and articulates the three volumes. The main pavilion for the couple parallels the river. A second volume, intended to house the children and their friends, is slightly inclined, to achieve space in the width of the site and to control the building's length.

The house uses the same site strategy as the Llu House, rising over the landscape on top of a steel pillar structure. An opening parallel to the house walkway takes people near the pillar, to a terrace and barbecue area. Thus, from the parking area, the home expands to the entire site, to receive friends or, on the contrary, is compressed for the more intimate use of the couple.

This is a low-budget house, resolved with a simple volume, worked in a single material for the walls and roofs. The dried-pine fuselage gives a dark tone, which blends very well with the environment. Inside, a very light color—from eucalyptus—makes a warm contrast with the exterior and provides lightness to the space.

The house's restrained and unpretentious profile allows the landscape to be the protagonist in dialogue with architecture. The space achieves its complexity using a double diagonalization of the two built-in architectural bodies. On the one hand, the roofs are diagonal at their ends, and on the other, the vertical ends form downward diagonals. This simple gesture is visible from the interior, giving volume and texture to the home. The final result is honest and gave the homeowners so much happiness that it became their primary residence.

* From the T House, designed in 2009 and built in 2011 on the banks of Laguna de Aculeo, a way of naming the projects was developed. It has to do with a synthesis of the architectural concepts that give life to space, generating an alphabet of forms. The concept speaks to the creation of reality through language. Each "letter house" has a unique dialogue with the landscape, a territorial dialogue where the work creates unity between landscape and architecture.

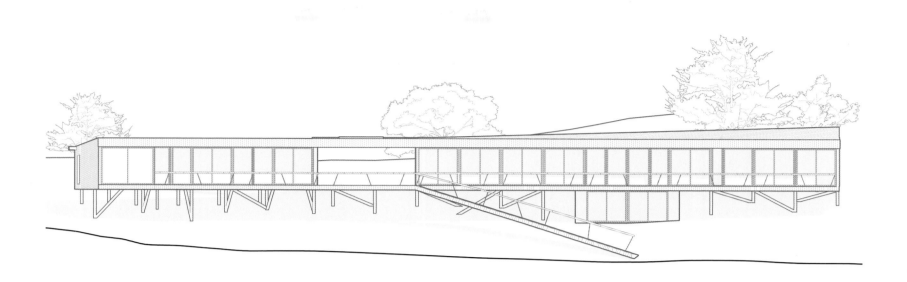

▲ **Elevation**

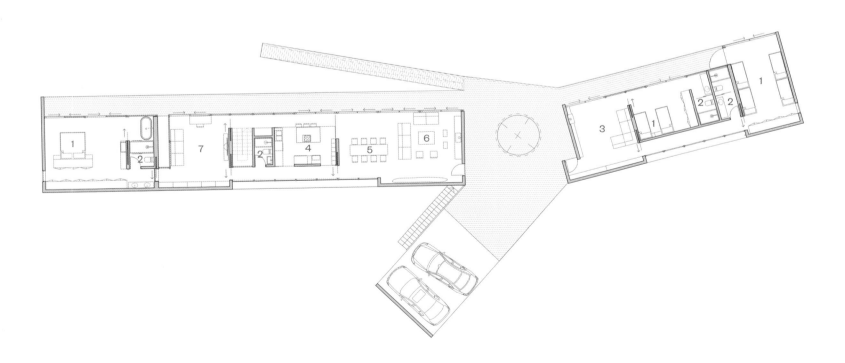

▲ **First Level Plan**
1. Bedroom / 2. Bathroom / 3. Living / 4. Kitchen / 5. Dining Room / 6. Living Room / 7. Desk

# Casa Lum

Lum House
2022

**Location:**
Catapilco
Valparaíso Region, Chile

**Collaborators:**
Isabella Massa
Carolina Wenzel

**Structural Engineering:**
Joaquín Valenzuela

**Lighting Design:**
Luz + Diseño
Gaspar Arenas

**Decoration:**
Vicky Cha

**Landscape:**
Magdalena Vergara
Joel Godoy

**Short Documentary Film:**
Diego Escobar

The owners, a middle-aged couple living in the countryside working with plants and essential oils, originated the concept of this house. The husband, a person of great humor, named the house "La Ultima Morada," therefore LUM. The name translates in English as "last resting place," but LUM works only in Spanish. He also had an idea of the form, and they planted and created the garden on-site, so I used his ideas and the garden as my starting points.

The spirals observed in plant growth and described by the Italian mathematician Leonardo Pisano Fibonacci (1140–1270) inspired the proportions of the garden and the site placement of the house. It is a serpentine pavilion related to the sunrise—for the wife's morning meditation—and all astronomical phenomena like the rising full moon and its relation to the distant hills. Each of these natural situations becomes a rite for their daily lives. In these everyday rituals connected to nature, the garden and the space allow them to enjoy life in a loving and substantial way.

The volume winds over a rock garden, made with pre-Columbian ceremonial stones protected by a semicircular rock fence and a layer of quartz, creating an intimate living space that centers on the axis of the primary Fibonacci curve of the house. The second curve, centered on the axis of the garden in the front yard, gives space to the entrance, located between the studio and house. In this way, the living area and bedroom can be used as a continuous private space if there are guests.

The roof controls the architectural curves, defining the volume with a diagonal ridge from one extreme to the opposite, creating a compact volume reinforced by the timber deck over the walls and roof. The interior walls are also worked as long curving lines. Hence, doors become invisible to reinforce the power of space, a tension that runs from the studio area located in the south to the main bedroom at the other end of the space. The use of cardinal directions was another request of the owners. This was not the best solution for the control of solar gain and climate efficiency, but it proved important to them. The area tends to flood in winter, so the entire volume was raised 15¾ inches (40 centimeters) above ground level, a practical solution that also creates a floating space open to the landscape. Columns supporting the roof come directly from the ground, supporting terraces from the outside and reinforcing the architectural idea of the floating pavilion.

The project is sustainable and low budget. We put much effort into confirming the energy performance of the walls, floors, and roof layers, using Passivhaus solutions, and protecting the space from the sun with externally covered corridors. These passageways also form an intermediate space open to the east and west. The quartz rock garden in the west, facing the sunset, was not a good solution in terms of climate efficiency, but, articulating the desires of the owners in an efficient and balanced way, it also ensures the coherence of the architecture.

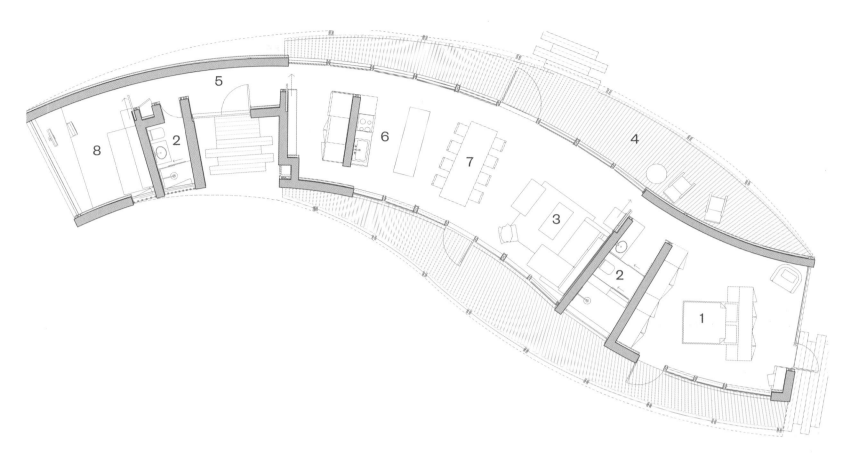

▲ **First Level Plan**

1. Bedroom / 2. Bathroom / 3. Living Room / 4. Terrace / 5. Access / 6. Kitchen / 7. Dining Room / 8. Workshop

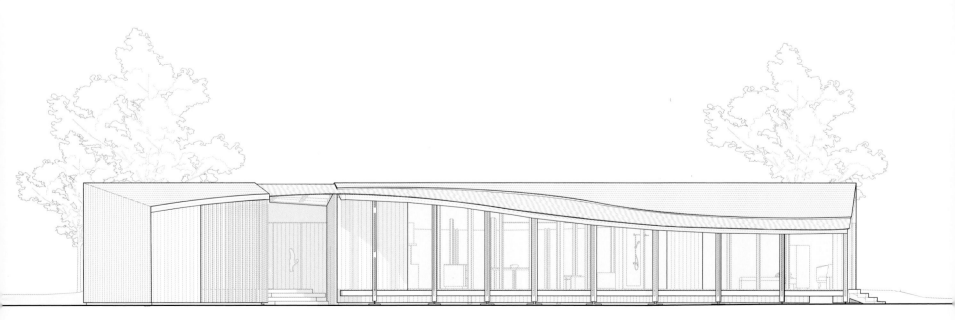

▲ **Elevation**

# Tierra Pata- gonia

Tierra Patagonia Hotel
2011

**Location:**
Sarmiento Lake (Torres del Paine)
Magallanes Region, Chile

**Associated Architects:**
Project Manager: Rodrigo Ferrer
Details: Roberto Benavente

**Collaborators:**
Juan Pablo Almarza
Gerardo Armanet
Carlos Cárdenas
Carolina Garrido
Juan Luis Ibañez
Nicolas Ramirez

**Structural Engineering:**
VPA
Enzo Valladares

**Lighting Design:**
Diseño de LUZ
Paulina Sir
Gaspar Arenas

**Decoration:**
Alejandra Edwards
Carolina Delpiano

**Artwork:**
Showcase: Matilde Huidobro
Map: Claudia Peña

**Landscape:**
Catalina Phillips
Gerardo Ariztía

**Short Documentary Film:**
Pablo Cassals

The hotel is located at the north entrance of the Torres del Paine National Park, on the edge of Sarmiento Lake, which forms the boundary of the park. The location has a grandeur that flows from the splendor of southern Patagonia. The vast panorama is generated by the water that acts as a support for the magnificent Paine Massif. The dimensions of this place, which can only be understood in metaphysical terms, led me to create an extended project anchored in a soft slope, which enters into dialogue with the magnitude of the territory.

Ecotourism of course happens in nature, but contemporary man is not equipped to live outdoors without protection. I wanted this building to be a second sensitive skin that allows visitors to experience the strength, beauty, and mystique of the place. The territorial gesture is a free body over the land, with arms defined as the geographic landmarks that form the shore of the lake and the limits of the land, the trails and roads which give access to the hotel might be compared to its legs. The head points to the Paine Massif, and the hotel is the heart. So, this project represents a love affair between landscape and free men.

The architectural gesture of the building originates in the poetic word *wind*, a strong presence in the topography of this territory, which is marked by slopes and dunes, elements carried by strong winds from the glaciers. The form of the building seeks to fuse with the landscape, emerging from the land on a slope and folding in on itself, with a fuselage of local timber that confronts the seasonal wind and generates a protected entrance area for visitors. The image of the hotel becomes that of an ancient fossil, some prehistoric animal stranded on the shores of the lake. (Travel to Patagonia played a role in allowing Charles Darwin to develop his theory of human evolution.)

The spatial solutions of the architecture seek to generate shelter and a human scale; these are structured by circulation spaces that link the public areas at the edges. Space for public gatherings is at the head for the plan, and at the end lie a pool and spa. In between, the forty rooms (both suites and standard) are organized on two levels. Doors are grouped together every two rooms, so the 656-foot (200-meter) corridor has pauses and a rhythm. On the first level, the artist Matilde Huidobro created three glass boxes telling the history of Patagonia. The second-level access to the rooms is resolved with small bridges that shape openings on the exterior slope to bring natural light into the space during the day. At night, the building appears like a vast lamp illuminating the darkness.

For me, the structure is always part of the architecture; in this case, the structure rests on beams that support the roof and the fuselage, created by local woodworkers. Each beam has a different shape corresponding to the double curvature of the building. I left the north wing open, to reveal the honesty of the structure. Roberto Benavente, in charge of the project detailing, solved the timber roof coating in a "light and precarious way."* He invented a concrete plot system to anchor the timber structure to the roof, a solution that did not require cutting the waterproofing membrane.

*Cazú Zegers

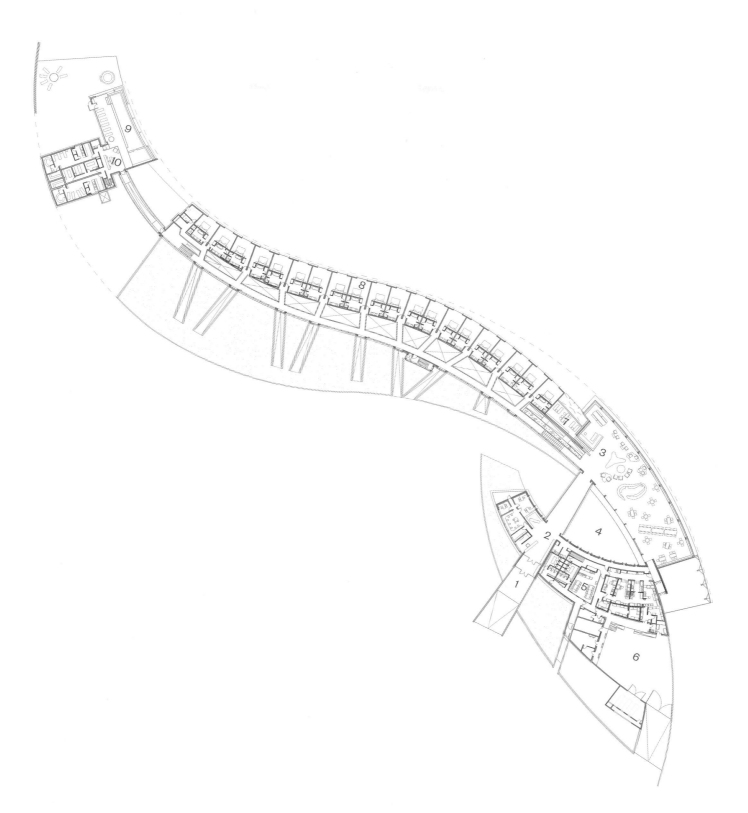

▲ **First Level Plan**
1. Main Entrance / 2. Reception and Store / 3. Living and Dining Room / 4. Patio / 5. Kitchen and Services / 6. Unloading Area /
7. Reading Room / 8. Rooms / 9. Swimming Pool / 10. Spa

▲ **Cut**

# Mag-
# nolia

Magnolia Hotel
2016

**Location:**
Santiago, Chile

**Associated Architects:**
Ian Hsü
Gabriel Rudolphy

**Collaborators:**
Isidora Urrejola
Sandrine Muñoz

**Structural Engineering:**
VPA
Enzo Valladares

**Lighting Design:**
Diseño de LUZ
Paulina Sir
Gaspar Arenas

**Decoration:**
Carolina Delpiano
Germán Margozzini

**Brand Design:**
Estudio Lila
Clara Larraín
Sofía Irarrazaval

**Boxes Artwork:**
Verónica Ibañez

The Magnolia Hotel was a restoration and an intervention project that sought to achieve a balance between the old and the new, memory and the present. It was a kind of echo of the past that arrived as a support for the contemporary. The biggest architectural challenge of this project was adding three new floors to an old building (listed as historical heritage) and consolidating a boutique hotel with forty-two rooms in the center of the city.

In order for the new to communicate coherently with history, we printed and installed a photograph of the original facade of the building on a glass surface that covers the three new floors. One of the main intervention strategies corresponds to the concept of what we call "illuminating the catacomb." The first three original floors already had little light, like other classic buildings of the 1920s, an issue that would be aggravated by adding three floors. Municipal regulations required that the new elements had to follow the same profile as the original building. We proposed to bring light to these first levels by opening up three existing patios. Two new stairs conceived as light wells were added around the elevator shaft, complementing glass corridors, thus generating sources of natural light capable of illuminating the entire building.

The intervention was consolidated with a generous inhabitable terrace that takes the user to a full view of the territorial environment, going well beyond a traditional viewpoint. From the terrace, guests and visitors have views of three mountain peaks near Santiago: Cerro Santa Lucía, Cerro San Cristóbal, and Cerro El Plomo, which represented a female deity for the Incas.

For the rooms, we proposed strategies to expand the space by blurring the limits, such as creating bathrooms that were part of the decoration, camouflaging them through translucent curtains or glass boxes that let light in without taking air out of the space. The original floor of the building was reused in the ceiling and wall cladding, leaving the existing brick exposed and introducing contemporary touches with bronze. The staircase, designed as a transparent metal sheet, runs through the construction.

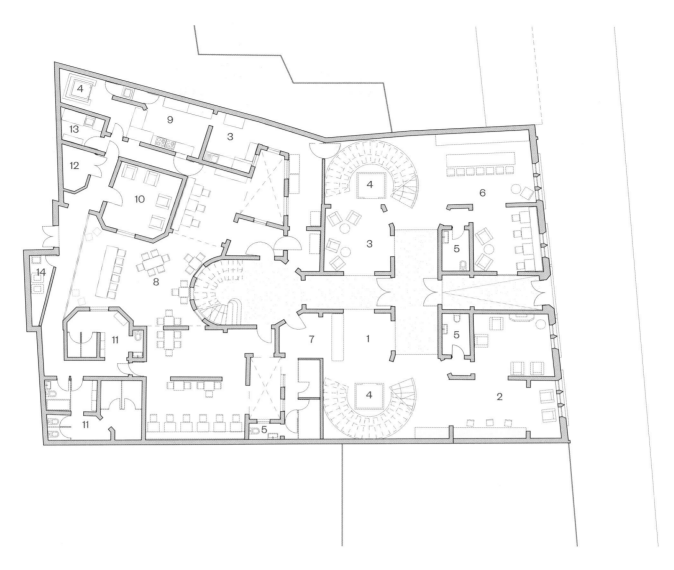

**▲ First Level Plan**

1. Reception Hall / 2. Living Room / 3. Living Room / 4. Elevator / 5. Bathroom / 6. Cafeteria / 7. Reception / 8. Dining Room / 9. Kitchen / 10. Service Room / 11. Dressing Room / 12. Technical Room / 13. Laundry / 14. Waste Collection

**▲ Elevation**

**▲ Cut**

# Casa Llu

Llu House Family Lodge
2018

**Location:**
Maihue Lake
Los Ríos Region, Chile

**Associated Architects:**
Ian Hsü
Gabriel Rudolphy

**Structural Engineering:**
VPA
Enzo Valladares

**Lighting Design:**
DIAV
Paulina Villalobos

**Decoration:**
María Luisa Zegers
Collaborator: Alejandra Franke

**Landscape:**
FAZ
Alejandra Sánchez
Francisca Sánchez

**Short Documentary Film:**
Clara Films
Producer: Clara Larraín
Director: Shawn Garry

This concept for a family lodge aims to house an entire extended group of relatives, including four generations and their friends, under the concept of hospitality. The Llu House is in the south of Chile, which is an extremely rainy area, a condition that evokes a poetic word for architectural design as *a cloak of protection from the rain*. This is a reference to the precarious tents that lumberjacks make in the forest with nylon stretched by wires, sometimes with a central pillar to let the water run down. This is the concept that is synthesized in Llu.

*Water* is the second poetic word that guides the design. This leads to the study of the geometric composition of water molecules;[1] thus, the idea of three bodies ($H_2O$) connected to each other guides the floor plan, which is made up of one level of space under a great blanket of protection against the rain, a cover made in handcrafted Corten steel. The need for a one-level floor plan combined with access ramps comes from the requirements of one of the family members, so the house had to be designed to permit disabled access.

The lodge is built on a structure of metal pillars, which take the shape of the site. The area below is used for services, as a protected area where the family and friends meet for alfresco lunch or parties, and where everyone can enjoy the hot tub.[2] Access and public space are located in the central part of the first level and connect bedrooms located in the two other lateral wings, which come together in the center in a smooth and fluid manner. Access to the bedrooms is through invisible doors to maintain the continuity of the walls and emphasize the spatiality of the volume without conventional corridors. Recycled native woods from old dismantled sheds and vernacular houses were used for the interior lining. This is a way of building a contemporary home anchored in tradition, and with reference to the iconic typologies of southern Chile. This recycled wood includes various types of native species, such as oak, raulí, coihue, and laurel, which give the walls a reddish hue, in perfect dialogue with the exterior of the fuselage. The floor is entirely made of raulí (*Nothofagus alpina*), and all the windows were constructed on-site with old pellín (*Nothofagus obliqua*) wood.

This mixture of vernacular and more recent typologies is carried out using contemporary language, favoring views of the place and its location within the broader territory. The language was achieved through canopies, linked to each other by the *cloak* of the geometric fuselage,[3] clad on the outside with handcrafted Corten steel plates that were prepared in situ, allowed to oxidize, and then sealed once they took on the desired color. The interior is worked, leaving the geometry of the cloak visible[4] and achieving heights of 16½ to 20 feet (5 to 6 meters), which gives the space nobility.

[1] Strategy from Emerald House.
[2] Location strategy from Emerald House.
[3] Concept that comes from Emerald House through the study of the geometric composition of emerald crystals.
[4] Action incorporated as a lesson from Emerald House, where the roof geometry is not made to appear inside, remaining as a wish for the future.

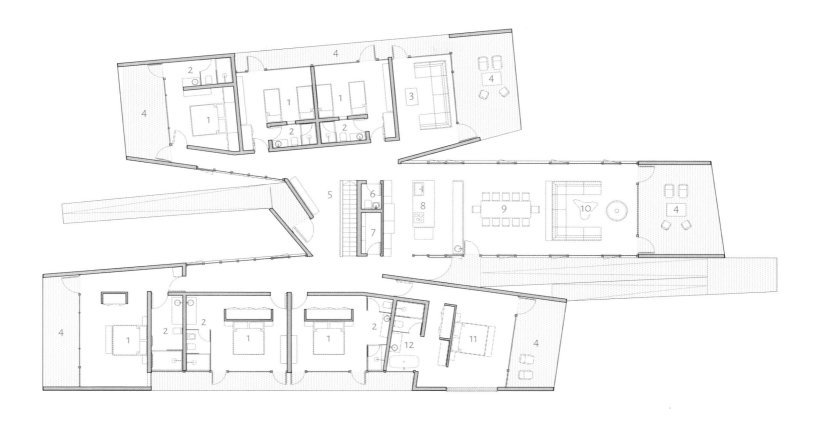

▲ **First Level Plan**

1. Bedroom / 2. Bathroom / 3. Living Room / 4. Terrace / 5. Entrance Hall / 6. Guest Bathroom / 7. Wine Cellar / 8. Kitchen / 9. Dining Room /
10. Living Room / 11. Master Bedroom / 12 . Main Bathroom

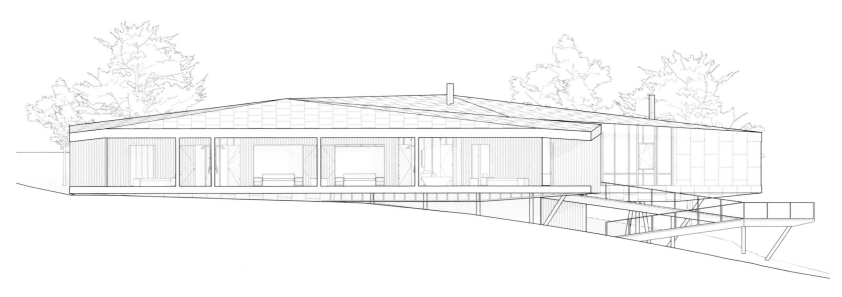

▲ Cut

# Casa del Fuego

House of Fire Family Lodge
1996/2020

**Location:**
Maihue Lake
Los Ríos Region, Chile

**Collaborator:**
Paola Vorgilli

**Structural Engineering:**
Joaquín Valenzuela

**Lighting Design:**
Diseño de LUZ
Paulina Sir
Gaspar Arenas

**Decoration:**
María Luisa Zegers

**Landscape:**
FAZ
Alejandra Sánchez
Francisca Sánchez

**Short Documentary Film:**
Clara Films
Producer: Clara Larraín
Director: Shawn Garry

The purpose of this house was to create a gathering place that could accommodate up to eight families simultaneously for a month or receive a single person in winter. The word *fuego* (fire) was used to name this house because it is in a territory of ancient volcanic eruptions. This is a land formed by fire, both ancient and powerful. Then, too, the origins of architecture can be found around the fire; the clan that gathers at the hearth builds its hut for protection. The architectural response to these ancient ideas is that of a family lodge structured around two volumes—the main house and the second volume to host the children.

The program is developed in three parts, connected and evolved around a center that determines the entire space. The fireplaces at the center of the house organize the family gathering places; from there, shells splay out in a centripetal way, giving place to the rest of the architectural program. The first shell from the center hosts the second-generation bedrooms, and the third volume is for the third generation and caregivers. The image evoked by this scheme is that of a spiral galaxy rotating in space, which emerges from the earth and reenters it; its speed loosens the shells that bind the three bodies of the interior space. The material is local timber worked in the traditional vernacular way. Curves were created using wet wood.

**Addition (2020)**
As the family grew, the fourth generation brought new requirements to the space, to host forty-seven family members with new couples. A new galaxy was formed from the initial one, as can be observed in the sketches for this project. The additional space requirements were resolved by transforming the old parking space, covered and open, into a protected circulation area where firewood is stored. This space articulates the new volumes with the previous house, a kitchen, and an outside living area for the family that assumes a circular form where existing trees are allowed to remain as a kind of *galaxy nursery* formed from the initial gesture. An inhabitable roof, on top of the living space, includes a hot tub and an area planted with grass for resting after the bath. On top of the kitchen and woodshed, the roof is covered with a timber deck, which offers a yoga space, connecting with the Llu House and the fourth-generation house through the second level. The space constantly flows through the circulation links and is not in any sense blocked. The inside area of the previous children's house was converted into master bedrooms and different living areas. This novel organization changed all the space use, centering family gatherings around the outdoor fireplace. The original program of the lodge expanded into the territory, with two separate houses for caretakers, a further house for the people who live on-site permanently, and in the middle, in front of the orchard, a place for laundry and seasonal employees.

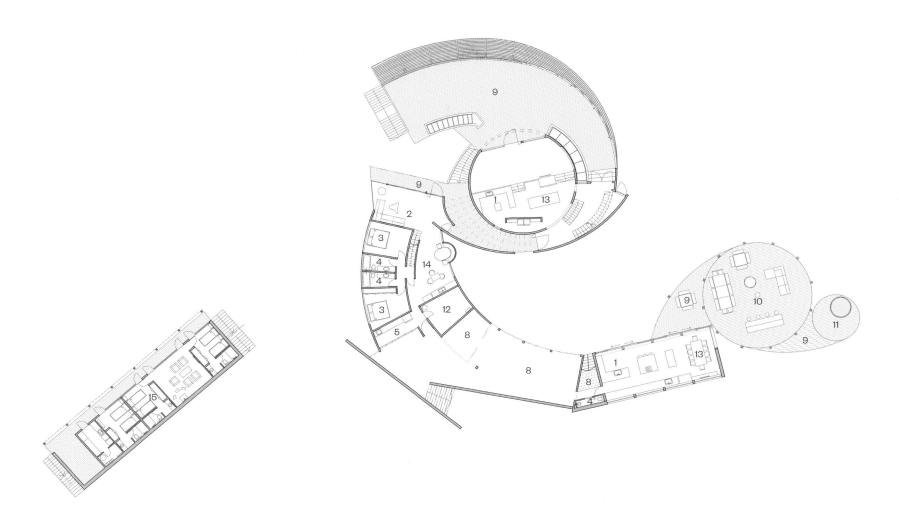

▲ **First Level Plan**
1. Kitchen / 2. Living / 3. Bedroom / 4. Bathroom / 5. Loggia / 8. Wood Cellar / 9. Terrace / 10. Barbecue / 11. Hot Tub / 12. Pantry / 13. Dining Room / 14. Kitchenette / 15. Service Pavilion

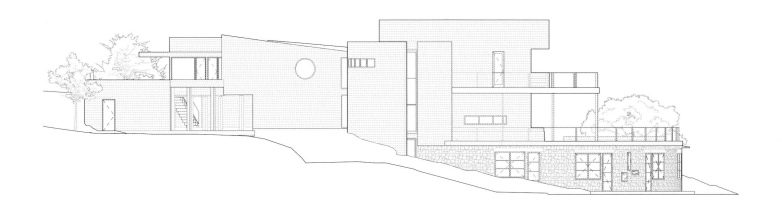

▲ **Cut**

# Casa Pyr

Pyr House Family Lodge
2023

**Location:**
Panguipulli
Los Ríos Region, Chile

**Collaborators:**
Francesca Fazzalari
Francisca Pereira
Carolina Wenzel
Joaquín Garin
Andrés Rengifo

**Structural Engineering:**
Joaquín Valenzuela

**Lighting Design:**
Antonia Peon

**Decoration:**
Carolina Delpiano
Pía Correa

**Landscape:**
Camila Tironi

The site for this project proved challenging, with the sun coming from behind the main view of the lake, an orientation that defines the architectural concept, together with the proximity of a 40-foot (12-meter) cliff. The house was designed according to these two conditions, as well as a poetic word—in this case, *pyrite*, which is known as the "home stone," or firestone.

The house is conceived around a central stairway that connects the top of the site to the lake level. This indoor stair was built with the cubic geometric structure of pyrite. This architectonic answer to all the challenges of the project brings out a complex volume of three stories in dialogue with the rock, the primary material of the site, a condition that gives beauty and character to the structure.

The first thought was to make use of a cross-laminated timber structure—a technology that was prevalent in Europe but very avant-garde in Chile—so we decided to work with an Italian manufacturer. CLT, however, turned out to be the wrong decision for such a degree of architectural complexity. But it was an excellent solution for the site's cliff; it could be used to make construction less invasive to the place and to shorten the construction time. The owners didn't like the more solid volume; they wanted something lighter, with large openings. CLT was, after all, not the correct solution for the house, so we used a more traditional steel building system with a longer process and more site intervention. The construction company broke stones for two months, abandoning the project concept of anchoring the volume in rock and suspending the rest of the volumes, losing the original idea of a light intervention. This kind of situation can happen when you are leading with prototypes.

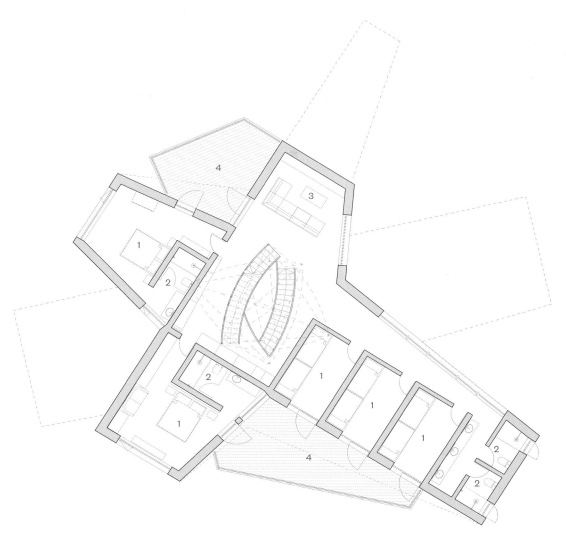

▲ **Bedroom Level Plan**
1. Bedroom / 2. Bathroom / 3. Living / 4. Terrace

▲ **Cut**

# Pueblo

Tiny House
2021

**Location:**
Lo Barnechea
Metropolitan Region, Santiago, Chile

**Collaborators:**
Francisca Pereira
Francesca Fazzalari
Isabella Massa
Alejandra Sepúlveda
Carolina Wenzel
Claudia Fuentes
Dominga Natho

**Structural Engineering:**
Cristián Sepúlveda

**Lighting Design:**
Cazú Zegers

**Decoration:**
María Luisa Zegers
Rosario Figueroa

**Landscape:**
Cristóbal Elgueta

The Pueblo project is a proposal for tiny, prefabricated housing designed in the form of a small town, with the aim of providing an attractive, high-quality living space at low cost. The urban area takes the shape of a pedestrian town, featuring small streets and squares surrounded by a sustainable natural environment. The project must react in a flexible manner, meeting the cost expectations of the client while satisfying the demands of future inhabitants. Quality finishing, thermal-acoustic comfort, privacy, efficient waste management, a friendly environment, good connectivity, and access to nearby hills are some of the goals.

The system of tiny houses is predefined in three sizes: 258 sq. ft. (24 m²), 527 sq. ft. (49 m²), and 700 sq. ft. (65 m²), assembled in sets of twelve units to create small neighborhoods. The goal is to reach six hundred units, which will include services such as cafés, gourmet stores, and bakeries. This would then form a cluster system that resembles a dense pedestrian town set in a park, offering stunning views of the Andean foothills of Santiago.

The concept for the urban planning is inspired by the form of trees, with the central street resembling the trunk and leading to a public space that serves as an open-air auditorium. The neighborhoods spread out like foliage, creating walkable side streets. The tiny, prefabricated system has transport limits that require the units to fit within a maximum width of 11½ feet and a length of 23 feet (3.5 × 7 meters). Despite this challenge, the design maximizes living comfort by using the vertical dimension to enlarge interior space, incorporating terraces, and connecting intermediate spaces through the assembling system. The exteriors of all the units are covered with a timber deck fuselage, providing a sense of unity and serving as a fifth facade for the neighbors who live higher up.

The complex is designed with high efficiency and sustainability standards in mind. Engineered timber is used as the primary material, known for its environmental credentials, as emphasized by the British architect Alex de Rijke. Unfortunately, the proposal was not selected because of concerns about the timber fuselage.

The concepts and sustainable systems developed for this project are now being reused as a starting point to create a prototype that aims to provide dignified, beautiful, and sustainable housing for poor communities. The project opens up possibilities for forming alliances with governments, communities, and industries to bring this vision to reality.

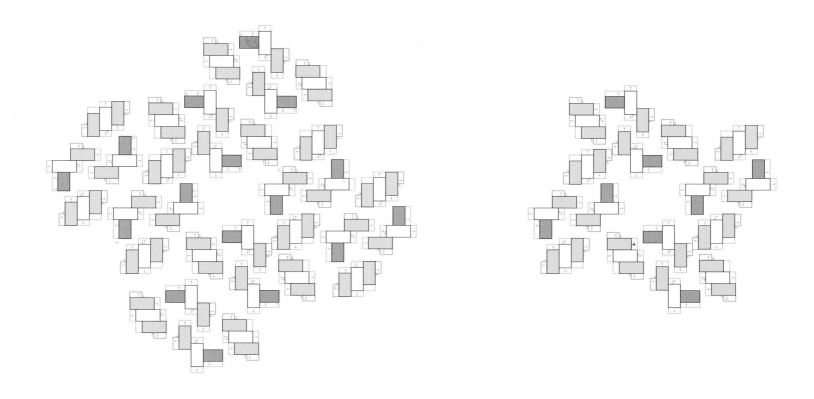

▲ Diagram of Module A and Module B grouping system

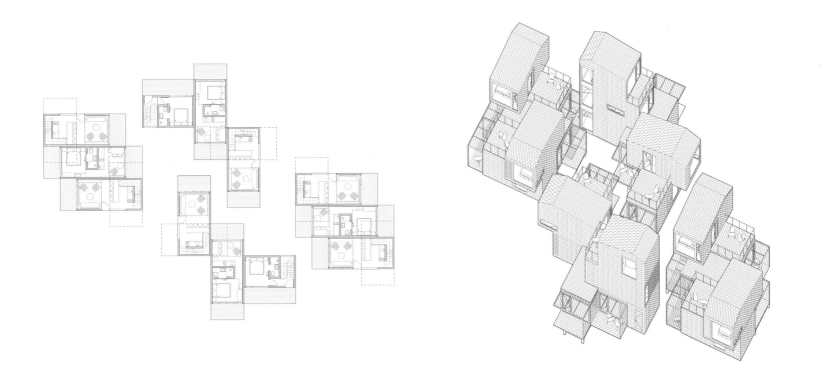

▲ A + B + C Scheme

# Acknowledgments

I would especially like to thank Philip Jodidio for trusting in me and encouraging the publishing of this book. His rigor and vision have undoubtedly led us to achieve a product of excellence. To my mother, Carmen García Dominguez, who gave me the wings which have taught me how to fly. To the artist and friend Gonzalo Pedraza, who helped me give shape and structure to this book.

To Colomba Cruz and Beltrán García for accompanying us on this adventure with love, rigor, and good disposition.

To the photographers of this book, Cristóbal Palma, Guy Wenborne, Cristina Alemparte, Juan Purcell, and Constanza Miranda, and a special thank to my dear nephew Marcos Zegers for his excellent work and disposition. Without a doubt their excellent photographic work allows us to create an object of great beauty. To my Head of Content at the studio, Josephine Tressler, who has done an extraordinary job of coordination for this project and of organizing and compiling the material for this book.

To my professors at the School of Architecture of Universidad Católica de Valparaíso, Chile.

To my current team at the studio: Francesca Fazzalari, Isabella Massa, Dominga Natho, and Clara Larraín for their work marked by excellence, and with whom we collaborate every day to give shape and beauty to the world. To my adventure companions at the Geopoetic Institute of Chile, *Fundación Observatorio de Lastarria/Fundación +1000*, and the educational and collaborative platform Andes Workshop.

To my Associated Architects, Rodrigo Ferrer and Roberto Benavente, for the Tierra Patagonia Hotel and Gabriel Rudolphy and Ian Hsü for the Magnolia Hotel, Casa Llu, and Casa Ye. And to each of the architects who have collaborated as well as specialists, builders, and engineers who have participated and, thanks to their excellent work, has helped bring these buildings to life. A special mention to my Studio Workshop Managers over the years, Andrea Pesqueira, Juan Pablo Almarza, Francisco García Huidobro, and Alejandra Sepúlveda.

I would like to give an enormous thanks to each of my clients over the years, who have trusted and believed in my work. Furthermore, thanks to the clients whose houses or projects have given life to this beautiful book, Pía Correa and Carlos Larraín (Pyr), Magdalena Vergara and Joel Godoy (Lum), Carmen García Dominguez (Fuego and Esmeralda), Victoria García Dominguez and Patrizia Pozzi (Llu), José Manuel Godoy (Ye), Inversiones Villanueva, José and Juan Pablo Villanueva (Magnolia), Katari S.A and Matetic Family and Miguel Purcell (Tierra Patagonia), Juan Forch and Francisca Vial (Do), Comunidad San Jerónimo, Sebastián Vial, Cristobal Lira, and donors (Capilla ES): I am grateful for your trust and the opportunity to make your homes and spaces a reality.

Special thanks to Rizzoli, Ellen Cohen, and Charles Miers.

Finally, to my daughter Clara Larraín Zegers and to my spiritual father and teacher, the poet Godofredo Iommi Marini, to whom I dedicate this book.

First published in the United States of America in 2024 by
Rizzoli International Publications, Inc.
300 Park Avenue South
New York, NY 10010
www.rizzoliusa.com

For Rizzoli
**Publisher:** Charles Miers
**Senior Editor:** Ellen R. Cohen
**Production Manager:** Alyn Evans
**Managing Editor:** Lynn Scrabis

For Cazú Zegers
**Production Manager:** Josephine Tressler, Sebastián Sottorff
**Collaborators:** Cazú Zegers Creative Ecosystem: Francisca Pereira,
Isabella Massa, Dominga Natho, Aranxa García, Sebastián Sottorff,
Josephine Tressler, José Domingo Smart, Clara Larraín, José Mercado

Designed by Colomba Cruz & Beltrán García

2024 2025 2026 2027 2028 / 10 9 8 7 6 5 4 3 2 1

ISBN: 978-0-8478-3400-6
Library of Congress Control Number: 2024935488

Printed in Hong Kong

Photographs:
Cristina Alemparte: p. 10, Lee Busel: pp. 221, 223, Collective Os
Espacialistas: p. 220, Loreto Mellado: p. 13, Constanza Miranda: p. 61,
Cristóbal Palma, Marcos Zegers: pp. 62, 87, 92–93, 98–99, 102–3, 144–45,
162–63, 166–67, 174–75, 190–215, Juan Purcell: pp. 84–85, Rodrigo Sheward:
p. 219, Guy Wenborne: p. 9.